AF873807

EDUCATION JUDO: HOW ASIANS CAN WIN THE COLLEGE & FINANCIAL AID GAME

By *Allen M. Leung, Esq. &*
Winnie H. Shiao, Esq.

Printed in the United States of America

ISBN 978-0-615-52519-8

Published by College Financial Aid,
A Division of Law Offices of Allen M. Leung
4000 Barranca Parkway, Suite 250
Irvine, CA 92604
www.PaylessCollege.com

If you know yourself and your opponent, you will be victorious in every battle against your opponent.

If you know neither yourself and nor your opponent, you will be defeated in every battle against your opponent.

If you just know yourself but not your opponent, or vice versa, then you will suffer one defeat for each victory against your opponent.

~ Sun Tzu, *Art of War*,
Approx. 2,500 years ago

Also by Allen M. Leung

Legal Judo: Strategic Applications of Reexamination Versus an Aggressive Adversary (Part I), 84 J. Pat. & Trademark Off. Soc'y 471 (June 2002)

Legal Judo: Strategic Applications of Reexamination Versus an Aggressive Adversary (Part I), 84 J. Pat. & Trademark Off. Soc'y 553 (July 2002)

About the Authors

Attorney-at-Law Allen M. Leung; Winnie H. Shiao, Attorneys-at-Law
Husband And Wife

Mr. Leung and Ms. Shiao are attorneys specializing in taxation and personal finance. In 2002, Allen M. Leung researched and developed a novel legal strategy that had a profound impact on the legal community. Mr. Leung outlined a strategy, named *Legal Judo*, on how the small inventor can fight and win against bigger corporations in patent battles. Since then, Mr. Leung's *Legal Judo* strategies have been cited often by many other lawyers and academics, and have had a lasting impact in the legal community.

Now Mr. Leung and Ms. Shiao are writing this book to shake up the education community the same way, specifically the Asian community. The challenge facing the Asian education community is how students could gain admission to top schools and receive financial aid. With this book, Mr. Leung and Ms. Shiao provide step-by-step strategies on doing so. Naming these strategies *Education Judo,* Mr. Leung and Ms. Shiao aim to astound readers that it is not so difficult for Asian students to attend premier colleges and universities, and receive financial aid as well. Well researched and backed by statistics, this book is unlike any other book on the market.

Mr. Leung and Ms. Shiao do not hold any formal belts in the martial art of judo. However, through their experience and knowledge, they are confident to say that they hold "black belts" in *Legal Judo* and *Education Judo*.

ACKNOWLEDGEMENTS

We want to acknowledge many family members and friends who have provided support for us during our writing process these past few months. When we hatched up the idea of writing this book a mere 3 months ago, we thought we would just write from a from a pure legal (tax) point of view. However, after conducting an informal survey, that pure legal point of view may be on the boring side. Thus, our book has evolved into education and financial aid perspectives.

We also like to thank our parents for their immense support. Winnie's Dad would be especially proud since he was an elementary teacher for 41 years. So it means a lot for him to see Winnie to write a book on education. Winnie also wants to thank her Mom for teaching her many street-smart tactics while growing up.

Allen wants to thank his Mom for cooking him fish soup almost daily while growing up. He also wants to thank his Dad for enthusiastic support and astute analysis for this book.

We are also very much indebted to the following individuals for their review, comments and encouragement: Janice Chen, Professor Jenny Yen, and Joann Hong. And to Alvinnie Kwok, a huge thank you for your work on the Table of Contents and Index. And you did it in such short time.

And to our two awesome daughters, Jocelyn Marie and Jacqueline Diana, for editing and checking numbers in detail throughout the book.

We could not have completed this book without everyone's help and encouragement. Thank you!

FORWORD

When we opened our older daughter Jocelyn's 6th grade yearbook recently, she had written that in 10 years, she wants to attend Brown University. Wow, we thought to ourselves. Perhaps we should think about how to get in to Brown, and how to pay for it. So we did some quick research and were absolutely astonished to find that the Cost of Attendance for Brown University is currently $60,000 per year. That actually enhanced their status as Brown received record number of application this year and had its lowest admission rate ever.

Being both lawyers, we researched some more, primarily reviewing the "Common Data Set" (CDS) of many schools. The CDS is submitted by colleges each year to the U.S. Department of Education, National Center for Education Statistics. Of course, the CDS is also relied upon heavily by magazines such as *US & World News* for its annual college rankings. The CDS provide in-depth statistics of each school and thus provides a much more clearer picture of a school than its own brochures.

Furthermore, by reviewing such objective and updated data, we can derive conclusions on what is the "best approach" to gain admission to that particular school. In another words, we are looking for each school's "weakness" that we can suggest students to attack. As you will see in the book in detail, every school has a weakness. We also can tell form the data whether a school is "generous" or "cheap" when it comes to financial aid.

As parents, we want to target those schools which our children can receive a great education, AND be able to obtain scholarships and/or financial aid. In another words, we want the best bang for our buck. At first, like many parents, we just wanted to focus on the Ivy League due to the aura of its "prestige." However, we discovered many other schools in our research journey outside the Ivy League that are "generous" AND offer a great education.

Thus, we have compiled a list of 68 schools and we are sharing their admission and financial aid profile. Why 68 schools? Co-author Allen Leung is an avid sports fan. Since we are on the topic of college, he picked the number 68 to coincide with the number of teams in the annual NCAA basketball tournament.

After the Ivy League, we divided the rest of the schools by geography or their athletic affiliations into "Conferences." For example, we group several schools from the NESCAC (New England Small School Athletic Conference) together with other elite liberal arts schools to form the "Little Ivies/NESCAC" Conference. Home to Williams, Amherst and Wesleyan, the NESCAC is like a smaller version of the Ivy League.

Moreover, we are writing from the view of California parents and students, balancing reputation and generous financial aid. Thus, we excluded many fine out-of-state public schools such as University of Texas-Austin, University of Michigan-Ann Arbor, and University of North Carolina-Chapel Hill. This is because CA residents would receive very little financial aid from these schools since they have to reserve most of their financial aid money to their own in-state students. Furthermore, we have left out some private schools that are also very good, because we are unable to profile every school. We are simply profiling schools that we believe CA students would most likely attend based on reputation, academics and financial aid.

The complete list of the schools is as follows:

Ivy League	**Little Ivies/NESCAC**	**West Coast Elite**	**East Coast Elite (Small to Mid-size)**
Brown	Amherst	Cal Tech	Barnard
Columbia	Bates	Claremont McKenna	Brandeis
Cornell	Bowdoin	Harvey Mudd	Bryn Mawr
Dartmouth	Colby	Pomona	Bucknell
Harvard	Haverford	Reed	Colgate
Princeton	Middlebury	Santa Clara	Lehigh
UPenn	Swarthmore	Scripps	Olin
Yale	Wesleyan	Stanford	Vassar
	Williams	Univ. of Pacific	Wellesley
		USC	

East Coast Elite (Mid-size to Large)	**Midwest Elite**	**Select UC's**	**Southern Elite**
Boston College	Carleton	Cal Poly-SLO	Davidson
Boston Univ.	Carnegie Mellon	UC-Berkeley	Duke
George Washington	Case Western	UC-Davis	Emory
Georgetown	Macalester	UC-Irvine	Tulane
Johns Hopkins	Northwestern	UCLA	Univ. of Richmond
MIT	Notre Dame	UC-San Diego	Vanderbilt
NYU	Oberlin	UC-Santa Barbara	
RPI	Rice		
Tufts	Univ. of Chicago		
	Wash U-St. Louis		

Note: We have *alphabetized* the schools within each Conference above. However, in the book, we may group the schools close to each other based on geography. For example, in "Midwest Elite," we are profiling Northwestern and University of Chicago next to each other, so parents and student can compare these 2 schools more easily. Another example is the Claremont Colleges, which we have clustered them together just like their physical location.

Note to Our Readers

Organization of this Book

In Part I, we will immediately introduce our secret strategies, including the concept of sports in American culture. Specifically, how sports can be used as leverage for gaining admissions into the best schools in America. We will also argue against the study of Business as an undergraduate major. We believe it has little or no value. Thus, we are attacking common myths in Part I, and offering solutions for entrance to the America's elite schools with excellent financial aid.

Part II is the main reference section, as each school is detailed with data from the school's Common Data Set. It is grouped into the Conferences above. For each school, we outline the specific strategy for getting in to that *particular school.*

Part III is all fun and games (literally). Here, just like the NCAA basketball tournament, schools "played" against each other based upon different factors of "generosity." There is heavily favored Columbia vs. liberal arts Haverford; Coastal titans NYU vs. USC; and Rice against Midwest rival Washington Univ. – St. Louis. These are just 3 of the intriguing "match-ups." Will there be an upsets like the real NCAA basketball tournament? Happy reading.

Contents

Part I – Secret Strategies

Part II – Profile of Each School

PART I: Secret Strategies

SECRET STRATEGY NO. 1: Apply Early Decision/Action

We believe Asian students should apply Early Decision ("ED") or Early Action ("EA") to improve chances to gaining admission to the Ivy League and top private schools.

First, we will explain the details of ED and EA. Whereas Regular Cycle admissions have deadline of January 1st, both ED and EA have the same deadline – November 1st. The school would provide a decision by December 15th.

ED and EA are set up to allow students to apply to their No. 1 choice only. Since the applications are "early", schools would have a chance to review the applications of students who really want to attend their top choice school.

There are big differences between ED and EA. Applying ED means you can choose one school to apply early. And if you gain admission to that school, you must attend that school and you must withdraw your other applications. Early Action means that you can apply early to a school, and if offered acceptance, you are *not* obligated to attend.

Now that makes EA appear to be more flexible, and most students would choose this route. But colleges created "Single College Early Action" (SCEA) just to confuse students and parents some more. SCEA means that if you are applying EA, you can only applying to one school (similar to ED). For example, Yale and Stanford both offer students the SCEA option. Thus, you *cannot* apply SCEA to both Yale and Stanford. You must choose one. And if you apply to Yale using SCEA, you cannot apply to Brown using ED.

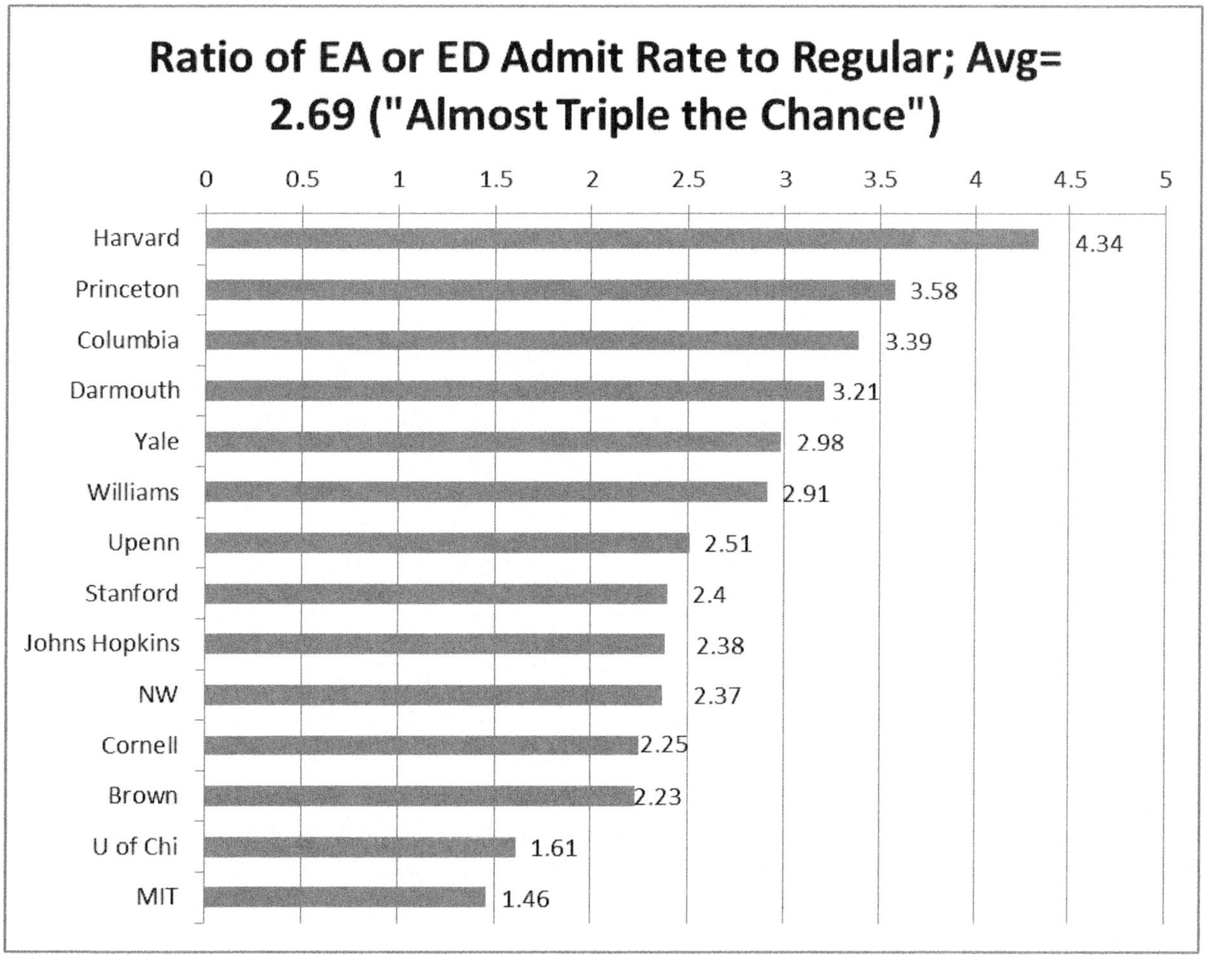

The above Chart clearly shows that ED/EA admit rates (HS Class of 2011) are *much higher* than Regular Admission. We have selected members of the Ivy League, Stanford, Northwestern, MIT and Univ. of Chicago (Harvard and Princeton do not have ED or EA.

So what does this mean? Take Harvard for example. It means your chances for admission to Harvard under ED is 4 times more likely than Regular (18% vs. 4%). For Princeton it is 3.58 times as likely to get in during ED than Regular (21.0% vs. 5.9%). The above 14 schools averages 2.69, which means if you apply ED or EA to any of the above schools, you chances for admission is more than *almost three time as likely* as Regular. Thus, the above serves as clear statistical evidence to apply EA or ED.

Can I apply to multiple schools using ED and EA?

Our answer for this is blunt and straight forward. *Don't even think about it.* It is just not worth it. If you apply for more than 1 school using ED and/or, that is lying on your application (The application would require the applicant to sign and attest to the fact that s/he would apply to only one school). If either one of the schools find out, you will be rejected even if you have perfect grades and test scores. No school would like to admit a student who intentionally lies.

How would they know? The admission officers in the Ivy League are in a small circle. Many of whom worked in different schools. For example, the Dean of Admissions at UPenn, Eric Furda, worked at Columbia at the same capacity. It would be easy for them to cross-check and identify any student who lied. This is part of academic integrity that all schools adhere to. A student who lies on the college application would violate this academic integrity and may even be "blacklisted" by other schools. Bottom line: just apply to one school ED or EA.

Conclusion

When a student applies for ED or EA, the school would provide 3 answers to the Applicant: (1) Admit, (2) Reject, or (3) Defer to Regular Cycle. If a student is rejected at the ED/EA cycle, that means s/he has no chance at the Regular Cycle anyway. If you get deferred, you are back to where you started anyway. Thus, you have nothing to lose by applying early.

Another way to view this is that if you don't apply early to top private school, your chance of admissions goes down by *more than 50%* (See Chart) in the Regular Cycle. If you get in by December 15th, your senior year in high school would be stress-free. While other students sweat and pray for admissions, you can relax.

SECRET STRATEGY NO. 2: Sports Culture in American Colleges

Sports is a big part of American culture, and sports is well integrated into college life. Asian parents and students need to understand this when applying to college. Participation in sports is another way you can contribute to your college.

Top academic colleges like Harvard, Yale, Princeton and Stanford take sports very seriously. For example, Harvard has a total of 39 teams for men and women, the most of any college in America. Each year, 600 new students out of the 2,000 enrolled participate in sports (30% of the freshmen class).

Thus, if you can play sports, that is another way you can "contribute" to Harvard. Why such emphasis on sports? Because it builds up school spirit. Harvard, Yale and Princeton have the most money among private colleges because of their strong alumni network, many of whom played sports when they were in college. This is another reason for Asian students to participate in sports – to develop connections with alumni (many who are CEO's or high level executives).

Harvard has a rivalry with Yale dating back 300 years, well before America declared independence from England. Neither team wants to "lose face" in any type of sporting competition. So both Harvard and Yale are looking for students (great academics of course) who can participate in sports. The students do not need to be Olympians. In most cases, they just need to be above-average "athletes" who have some training in high school.

Why? Because for most schools, they are just looking to "fill" their teams with competent athletes. This is especially true for schools that do not have much of an athletic tradition (i.e. MIT, Cal Tech). If you can exhibit some above average skills, it would help you application immensely. We would actually say that Asian athletes would be an advantage because there are so few of them in college (less than 1%). There you have it, if you are looking for an advantage to get into top school, show off your athletic skills.

SECRET STRATEGY NO. 3: Using Sports As Leverage in College Applications

Since college sports is imbedded in the American culture, then student-athletes have leverage in the college application process. So how can one use sports to gain acceptance, especially into the elite college such as Ivy League?

First, we are assuming you are an excellent student (e.g. high unweighted GPA, minimum 2,150 SAT or 32 ACT). These numbers may be higher for individual schools. And then if you are a "good" athlete, we are going to show you how you can translate that into an acceptance into a high-ranking school.

If you are "good enough," you would be noticed by the school's coaches. (Please also see our special section of Particular Sports related to how good you need to be). The term to use here is "recruited." In another words, the coach want you to be on the team. The following is a good way of thinking on how good you need to be: You need to be good enough to be recruited.

Coaches Submit Your Application to Admission Office

Once you are recruited, the **coach will submit the application** for you to the Admissions office. Let's take a step back. If you are a non-athlete, you are in the "general" application pile, where 9 out of 10 students are rejected in top private schools. But if you are an athlete and your grades are good (75 percentile of tests scores), your application just went into a "special" line. It goes without saying that applications have a much higher chance of admission.

Student-Athlete Admission Rate Much Higher Than Regular

In fact, we estimate that application sent in by coaches have a least a 45% of admissions. As mentioned, the top private schools have an admission of less than 10%. Thus, for student-athletes, your chances just went from 10% to 45%. That is what is meant by leverage into top schools.

Furthermore, there is shortage of Asian student-athletes in college sports. Thus, Asian student-athletes whose applications are submitted by coaches have an even *higher* chance of admission.

Our observation is that many Asian parents and students are always attempting to score that extra 50 points on the SAT, or squeezing 2 more AP classes in. We feel that there is a decreasing marginal return with this type of strategy. Scoring 50 extra points on the SAT has no guarantee of admission into top private or UC schools. You would be better off improving your athletics skills (i.e. putting, sprinting, serving, etc.).

Is It Fair?

Now we know that there are high achieving students (all ethnicities) who don't think it is fair that athletes receive special treatment. It is not our intention here to debate whether it is fair or not. Rather, we are writing this book to inform readers the truth. And since college sport so imbedded in American culture, special treatment to student-athletes is not going to change any time soon. Thus, we must embrace it and see how students can benefit from it. One thing for sure, there is shortage of Asian student-athletes in college sports. Just knowing this fact and the coach's role in admissions would increase Asian student athletes chances immensely.

College Sports in Different Divisions

Let's have an quick overview of different division in college sports. Division I schools (most competitive in sports) are those that offer athletic scholarships (i.e. it is a student's job to play sports). Examples of Division I schools with athletic scholarship are Stanford, USC, Duke, Notre Dame and Boston College. Division III (least competitive in sports) do NOT offer athletic scholarships, and student-athletes "come and go" as s/he pleases. Examples of Division III schools in book are Williams, Amherst, Pomona, MIT, and University of Chicago.

What about the Ivy League? It is actually in Division I, but they do *not* offer athletic scholarships. Since many Asian students are not really seeking athletics scholarships (and we are not recommending them either), that actually works very well in their favor. We are advocating that the student gets easier admissions through participation in sports—regardless if the student receives a scholarship. Once you gain admission into the school, continued participation in sports is *voluntary.*

Why Would the Coach Recruit Me, Since I am not at National Level?

This is one of the most false myths out there. Let's look at it from a point of a view of coaches whose schools don't offer sports scholarships (i.e. Ivy League, elite liberal arts schools, MIT, University of Chicago, etc). Put simply: the coaches need to "fill" their teams. Why? Well, each year, there are seniors graduating. The juniors are studying abroad. Some of the sophomores have quit (see below). Where is the biggest source of athletes for their team? Answer: incoming freshmen.

Remember participation in sports in these schools is *voluntary*. The school cannot force you to participate, even if you are recruited to play. And yes, some students apply through the coach to get in to a school, and then quit after the first year. In fact, this "get in first and quit later" strategy is common in elite colleges. Thus, the coaches need to fill team rosters with more than enough 1st year students, in anticipation of athletes leaving the team. This is particularly true for sports such as cross-country, track, swimming, crew, water polo and even football. Therefore, many coaches are not looking for national level athletes.

Conclusion

If there is one thing a reader can gain from this book, it is the fact that sports can help you gain acceptance to the top schools in America. By working with coaches, your application will submitted through a special "line" where admission rates are much higher. For Asian student-athletes, the admission rate would be even higher. We urge students of all ethnicities to take advantage of this special "line."

SECRET STRATEGY NO. 4: Particular Sports to Focus On

So how good do you need to be, and what sports should Asian students concentrate to maximize the sports leverage? Again, we are analyzing from the perspective of Asian students from California.

Football (Quarterback) for Males & Sprint Freestyle (Swim) for Females

If we have to choose which sport for Asian students to focus on that would result in almost "sure" ticket to the Ivy League and elite liberal arts schools, we would say football (quarterback) for males and sprint freestyle (swim) for females.

We would expect many readers to shake their heads and disagree with the above suggestion. Many Asian parents do not wish their sons to play football because of possibilities of injuries. Furthermore, many Asian parents and students do not believe Asian females can do well in sprint freestyle swimming.

One reason we are writing this book to tackle stereotypes and myths within the Asian community. Let's take one sport at a time. Why football? Because it is the all-American game. Participating in football by Asians shows integration into the mainstream society. And quarterback is the leader of the team.

Asian students are often viewed as lacking leadership by the top schools. What better way to defeat this myth than be a quarterback, the leader of a sport that is *quintessentially American*? In one move, your son would stand out from the average "Asian" pile and leap into the "football" pile with leadership qualities.

Back-up Quarterback

For those parents who worried about their sons getting injured in football, we have a solution. You can be the 3rd or 4th back-up quarterback, who rarely plays. But you are a team member. Thus, these back-up quarterbacks are probably the "safest" position on the football team.

So how do you become a back-up quarterback on an Ivy League team? Throw the football 50 yards, which can be done if by practicing and planning ahead. The Ivy League has not seen an Asian back-up quarterback for a long time. We are confident that coaches would welcome such an Asian team member. Since there are so few Asian football players in the Ivy League, let alone quarterbacks, we believe the athletic ability for such quarterback does not need to be too high. Specifically, if someone can throw the football 50 yards, then coaches in the Ivy League would at least consider you for a back-up quarterback position. And keep in mind the football coach has the most influence in admissions. If the football coach wants you for back-up quarterback, you are in.

Female Sprint Freestyle

Our suggestion for females is sprint freestyle in swimming, which directly contradicts many Asian parents' thinking that their daughters are not as good as other ethnicities in sprints. To understand our suggestion better, let us view from the coaches point of view.

In Ivy League and elite liberal arts schools (Amherst, Williams, Pomona, Swarthmore, Wellesley, etc), the most important swim meet is the conference championship at the end of the season. And for this meet, there are many sprint relays, mostly freestyle. (Each relay has 4 swimmers). Thus, swim coaches need female swimmers who can swim multiple freestyle relays. Consequently, if you are only good in breaststroke but not freestyle, you are not "useful" to the coach. Furthermore, relay points are doubled in the championship meet. Thus, the team that wins the relays can win the championship. That is why if you need to be good in one stroke, it should be in sprint freestyle.

Again, keep in mind many swimmers in the Ivy League and Little Ivies "come and go" each year (i.e. graduation, study abroad, quit, etc.). Thus, a swim team always needs freestyle sprinters.

How Fast in Sprint Freestyle?

Thus, if a CA female swimmer has attained Junior Olympic ("JO") time standards for age 15-16 in sprint events, then she would be a very attractive athlete to Ivy League and elite liberal arts schools.

Particular Sports (East & West Coast Bias)

Many Eastern coaches (Ivy League, top liberal arts schools) have certain bias in favor of sports that originated or are popular from the East. For example, lacrosse was invented by the Native Americans in present day New York state. Thus, Ivy League and liberal art schools favor lacrosse athletes from the East (almost exclusively). Although lacrosse is also popular in CA, coaches in the East discount (unfairly) the skills of CA lacrosse players (all ethnicities). Therefore, Asians student-athletes concentrating in lacrosse would not have a good "return" when applying Ivy League or the Little Ivies.

Furthermore, field hockey, fencing and squash are all additional example of sports where an Eastern bias exists (i.e. the belief that athletes from the East Coast are simply better in those sport). Fencers on the Ivy League, for example, usually include Olympians and National champions. The West Coast just do not yet have that fencing culture.

West Coast Sports (Water Polo & Swimming)

How about sports that students-athletes are view in high regard from East Coast coaches? Water polo and swimming comes to mind immediately because athletes participating in these 2 sports can train year-round in CA due to the fine weather. Many members of the U.S. National Water Polo team (men's & women's) are from CA. Thus, Ivy League coaches respect CA water polo athletes and water polo teams are filled with CA students. Thus, the fact that you play water polo in CA – the strongest competition in the country – would be instant credibility to a coach.

Swimming is also another sport where CA student-athletes are view favorably by East Coast schools. The time standards and competition in the West Coast are higher those in the East, particularly in women's swimming. For example, according the website of Wellesley (ranked 4th in *U.S. News* in Liberal Arts), the top 4 female times in 50 yard freestyle average about 25 seconds. There are many 13-14 girls in CA who can do this (According to usaswimming.org, forty-one aged 13-14 girls in CA have done that in 2011).

Conclusion

This chart will summarize the sports to focus on.

Sports that CA Students Should Focus in High School	Sports that CA Students Should Avoid in High School
Water Polo	Lacrosse
Swimming	Field Hockey
Tennis	Squash
Golf	Fencing
Soccer	Ice Hockey
Track/Cross Country	Crew
Football	
Softball	

SECRET STRATEGY NO. FIVE: 4.5 Sec Speed > 4.5 GPA

What does this statement mean? Many parents and Students ask us whether a 4.5 GPA is good enough to get admitted into the Ivy League, Stanford, MIT and/Cal Tech? A 4.5 GPA *used* to be a sure ticket for admission into such prestigious schools. But no longer.

We usually respond by staying is you have 4.5 (sec) speed, you have a much better chance. And we get nothing but blank looks on the face of parents and students. As we discussed in the previous sections, sports in big in American culture and many schools need student-athletes to fill their teams. For the most part, you just need to be an above-average athlete and you would have an advantage.

A "4.5 speed" refers to the time someone can run in a 40 yard dash. So 4.5 speed = 4.5 seconds in 40 Yards. It is most commonly applied to athletes to are in the NFL (National Football League). Now we are not saying your son and daughter should play football (although that helps a lot) to gain an edge.

College track teams have 60 meter sprints. So a 4.5 speed in 40 yards translates into approximate 7.2 seconds in 60 meters. That time would allow you be a contributing member of the track team.

For girls, the suggested speed is 4.7 sec, which would translate into approximately 7.80 sec for 60 meters. Thus, having a "4.5 speed" is most valuable than a 4.5 GPA (sorry but that is the truth). Is a "4.5 speed" out of reach for most Asian students? We think not. Some students are naturally quick and fast. It just takes some training and it is possible.

SECRET STRATEGY NO. 6:
Participating in College Sports Team

So far we have discussed in detail how sports can be used as leverage into the top schools. The next issue is the benefits and drawbacks of joining a sports team in college.

Many Asian parents, particularly the first generation, are dead-set against their kids playing sports in college. They believe that their sons and daughter should study hard and not "play."

We wish to counter that by stating you are not going to college just to study 24/7. One reason to attending prestigious school is to develop your own personal network of friends. Thus, if you study all the time, it would be hard to make any friends. Many Asian parents want their children to attend top schools so they can have a great career.

College Sports Will Help Your Career

If that is the case, then we strongly advise you join a sports team because it *will help your career*. Many Asian students attend the Ivy League each year as a springboard into Wall Street, investment banking and the business world. As many may know, the business world and Wall Street is full of personal relationships. It would be hard for outsiders to break in.

One way to stand out is sports participation. As we mentioned, sports in ingrained in the American culture. Many power brokers and "big shots" on Wall Street play sports when they attended Ivy League and other top schools. Thus, if you play sports in the Ivy League, you would immediately stand out.

Why? Because you have contributed to your school. Many top leaders on Wall Street really love their alma mater, and since you contributed to their school, you would be the first one to be hired for internships or permanent positions. Furthermore, participating in college sports means you are a "team player," an important concept when trying to break into Silicon Valley or Wall Street.

Thus, if you are the Asian quarterback from Harvard, that would just open up so many doors for you from Silicon Valley to Wall St. It doesn't matter that you rarely play. The fact that you are a team player and contributed to the school matters more than your grades.

Participation in Team Will Help Your Grades

Many Asian parents might not realize it, but participation in a college sports team will also help students' *grades*. How? Athletes have privileges. Thus, they would be allowed on campus before the general orientation. Thus, the team serves as an immediate social network for the new members. The captains of the team are obligated to take care of the incoming freshmen, as they were when they were new students. For example, the captains and upperclassmen would advise the new members on the "easy" classes and nice professors, the best places to eat and study etc.

The best part of joining a team is actually to make sure the student *goes to class*. If a team member does not attend a class, the professor would inform the coach, who would subsequently yell at the student. Therefore, the coach is like an surrogate parent who make sure the team members attend classes. For those parents who want their kids to study and study some more, how can you be sure that your son or daughter is actually going to classes? Answer: you cannot tell for sure. But joining a sport team would make sure that (s)he goes to class. Finally, tennis or swimming teams in the Ivy League usually have higher GPA than the average student body population.

Academic Advisor to Monitor Each Athlete

Furthermore, each team has an academic advisor, who keeps track of academic progress of all team members throughout the school year. For example, if someone receives a C on a test, the advisor would seek out the student and help him/her raise the grade. If your son or daughter receives a C on a test, would you the parent be informed? No, because schools consider students to be adults and do not notify the parents of any grades.

Also, athletes have priority in registering for classes. Thus, when the rest of new student finally show up for freshmen orientation, the 1st year sport team members has already made new friends (upperclassmen), registered for classes, know where everything is on campus, etc. The 1st year sports members may even be laughing at the new students. In other words, 1st-year athletes have become experienced students, just by joining a team.

Conclusion

Thus, sports can help you gain admissions, obtain better grades and facilitate your career goals. If you really do not like it after one year, you can quit because you are not under any obligations to continue. Therefore, with all these benefits and such flexibility, Asian student-athlete should consider joining sports team of their dream school.

SECRET STRATEGY NO. 7:
Math > Business As Undergrad Major

Take a look at AP Calculus Classes in Southern California (and Northern CA as well), and what do you see? Mostly likely many Asian students taking advanced, college-level math courses as a badge of honor.

And then when these advanced math (Asian) students go to college, do they study Math as major? No, by a long shot. Stanford has only 3% of its undergrad students studying Math (all races/ethnicities). How about USC? Only 1%.

What happened? A closer look shows the most popular major at USC is Business (26%). Again, that is compared to 1% in Math. How about MIT? Surely it must be a "hot" major since MIT is known for math/science. Well, only 10% major in Math at MIT.

Thus, it appears that Business is the "cool" college major and Math is not. Many students (and parents) believe that studying business in general as an undergrad will lead them straight to Wall Street, where bonuses are paid in the millions per year, year after year.

Undergrad Business Degree has Little Value

Let us make a statement regarding this approach, and perhaps after the shock wears off we can discuss it rationally. Our statement is as follows: *"The market does NOT think very highly of an undergraduate business degree."* (And that's being polite).

Why Business has practically no value? Simply because business skills are accumulated through experience and maturity. (Actually many Asian parents who are businessmen can understand this). So we issue the following challenge to any college student majoring in business: If you think you can take on Google, Apple, Yahoo, Mircosoft, etc, just by studying business, you can quit school, set up a company and compete with these "big boys" right now. (We are attorneys and we can even set up companies for you).

Business Icons but Did Not Studied Business

That was the path taken by Bill Gates, Steve Jobs and Mark Zuckerberg. Furthermore, for the following Internet companies, how many of their founders studied business as major at college?

(1) Google;

(2) Apple;

(3) Yahoo;

(4) Facebook;

(5) Microsoft.

The answer is **zero**. Sergey Brin of Google studied that "uncool" major of Math in college. Jerry Yang of Yahoo studied Electrical Engineering (which has a lot to do with math). The other three (Bill Gates, Steve Jobs, Mark Zuckerberg) attended some college but did not graduate. None of these three business icons studied business. Business people? They worked for these visionary leaders.

Thus, the leaders at Apple and Google are losing very little sleep at night worrying about 21-22 year old business graduates. Why? Because they know these business graduates pose very little "threat" to them. What they are really worried is the next "Steve Jobs" or "Mark Zuckerberg", who would invent the "next new thing" and compete with them.

Finance?

Then what about finance as a major, where students can graduate and go to Wall Street, and practice stock and bond trading? Let us answer that by asking an honest question. Would you entrust your hard-earned money to freshly minted college graduates to trade? There are programs of study tailor toward Wall St. (e.g. financial engineering). But it is in graduate school and not undergrad. With the exception of UPenn's Wharton School, undergrad business finance is just not respected in the market place. We do not like to be the "messenger" of bad news. But parents and student should know this before they spend $100K to $200K on an undergrad education with very little return.

HYPS Do Not Offer Business Major

Finally, consider this. If Business Administration is such an "important" undergrad major, how come Harvard or Stanford does NOT offer it? Neither does Princeton or Yale. Is it because they (as leaders of American education) know that business for undergrads is perhaps not valuable? If aspiring students want to study business, they should do it at the graduate level (i.e. MBA), after several years of industry experience.

We do, however, cite an exception to our rule above. If an international student just want to come to the U.S. for a business degree and then return home, then that is fine. This is because a U.S. degree carries enormous weight, especially in Asia.

Why Study Math?

Getting back to Math, we believe Asian students should study more because they are generally very good in math. The overall theme of this book is using your strengths to achieve your goals. Furthermore, math is an excellent "fundamentals" major. Specifically, Math can allow you to "springboard" to career such as business, computer science and engineering. And if you major in Math, you will receive excellent personal attention, due to the fact so few students study it. Again, let's review the education path of Sergey Brin, founder of Google, Inc. He studied Math in college and obtained a Masters in Computer Science (CS).

Follow Sergey Brin's Path

Why Math first and then CS? Because CS programming is mainly based on math algorithms. If a student understands these algorithms well, CS is a breeze. If the founder of Google walked this path, shouldn't more students follow suit? (By the way, Sergey Brin's father is a math professor)

We are not saying that by studying Math and the CS, you will establish the next Google for sure. What we are saying is that just by following this path, you would have a great chance for high-paying job at companies like Apple and Google. A much better chance than a plain business degree.

Finally, with an undergrad Math degree, you can obtain a Ph.D. in Math or Masters in Financial Math. With those advanced degrees, then you can go to Wall Street to obtain those million-dollar bonuses. Thus, Math will allow you to achieve your goal, rather than business degree.

SECRET STRATEGY NO. 8: Be Cool – You are From California

Growing up New York City, co-author Allen Leung had a simplistic view of West Coast: CA = Cool. For many Americans in the East, they also agree with the above formula, including admissions officers from the Ivy League and Little Ivies. Indeed, the whole world is infatuated with California culture, dating back to the popular song "California Girls" by the Beach Boys in 1965. Pop Singer Katy Perry currently also has a hit song with the same name, and thus reinforcing the idea that "CA = Cool." In both songs, the phrase "we wish all girls are CA girls…" are repeated often. Thus, CA students applying to the Ivy League and East Coast schools should have some sort of "coolness" in their application to confirm the admission officers' pre-conceived notions.

Show Coolness, Will Stand Out

So how should Asian students use "CA cool" to their advantage? We have the solution: just engage in activities that are considered "cool" but doesn't take too much time. For example, how many CA Asian students applying to top schools have joined Jr. Lifeguard program in the summer? Probably not many but you should. Reason: CA Lifeguard = Cool.

The TV show "Baywatch" was a huge hit in the 90's as it glamorized beach life in CA. Recently, the reality show "The O. C." further reinforced California coolness. And both males and females can join the Jr. Lifeguard, with programs in many cities in Southern CA. Thus, if East Coast schools expect CA applicants to be "cool," you must try to at least live up to such expectation.

What is "Uncool" to the Ivy League and Stanford?

A typical "uncool" applicant is someone who takes the SAT 3 times (only to improve 30 pts), take 7 AP tests (receive a 5 on only 1 of them), scores well on Math/Chemistry/Bio of SAT II and native language (Chinese or Korean), no sports and certainly no lifeguard, participates in about 10 clubs but not a leader in any of them, etc. There is nothing "cool" about this application at all. Since Harvard and Stanford cannot say this is "uncool", we will say it for them.

We are not against studying for the SAT or AP all summer. But are you really going to list "study for SAT test" as a summer activity on your Harvard application? So we are suggesting you engage in some "cool" activity for half the summer and then study the SAT for the other half. Thus, rather than studying the SAT for the entire summer, you can be a Jr. Lifeguard for 4 weeks, and then study the SAT for 4 weeks. That would allow your application to be suddenly "cool."

Projecting a Cool Image in Interview

All Ivy League and other top private schools now use interviews as part of the admission process. (Disclosure: co-author Allen Leung was an alumni interviewer for Cornell). When applicants to these top schools interview, they also need to come across as "cool" to the interviewer. What is that cool image? If an applicant has a slight CA sun tan, confident, and well-spoken, that applicant would stand out immediately because s/he projects a cool image. We also suggest the applicant talk about surfing in the essay and in the interview to reinforce the notion of "coolness." But how Asian applicants really try to project that image? To our knowledge, not many. And if your applicant oozes "coolness," your chances into the top schools just got a whole lot better.

PART II: Profile of Each School

CONFERENCE ONE: Ivy League

Each year, the Ivy League schools' admission rate keeps decreasing. Many students, especially Asian, complained that even though their "numbers" are better than the 75 percentile of a Ivy League but still are rejected. Out of frustration, many are mystified at the admission process and some even claim discrimination. So let us look at the data and see what is the best way to gain acceptance into the Ivy League.

Rather than just looking at the test scores of Ivy League schools, we iterate that there is a ***specific*** approach to each school based upon the data. Furthermore, you must use all your strengths and intangibles to your advantage, in addition to the usual test scores and GPA.

Ethnicity Disclosure & Race Unknown

Taking a look at Harvard, we see the ethnic percentage for whites and Asian as 44% and 17%, respectively. And we also see something very curious: 14% of Harvard students are "race unknown." Are you telling us that all of a sudden, 1 out of every 7 Harvard students somehow "forgot" their race and ethnicity? That makes no sense whatsoever.

Since the authors are lawyers, we are here to provide a very plausible explanation. Federal law allows students not to state their race or ethnicity if they choose in college applications. Thus, we suspect that many of these 14% Harvard "race unknown" students are actually white or Asian because they fear that indicating white or Asian would "hurt" their admission chances. Their college admission "coach" probably made such suggestion.

So let's assume half of these 14% Harvard "race unknown" students are actually Asian, then Harvard's Asian population would be close to one-quarter (24%=17%+7%). Keep in mind that the Asian population in the U.S. is only 5%. Thus, it would be hard to say that Asians are discriminated from this point of view. To be fair, Harvard students are not the only ones playing this "game." Please see below:

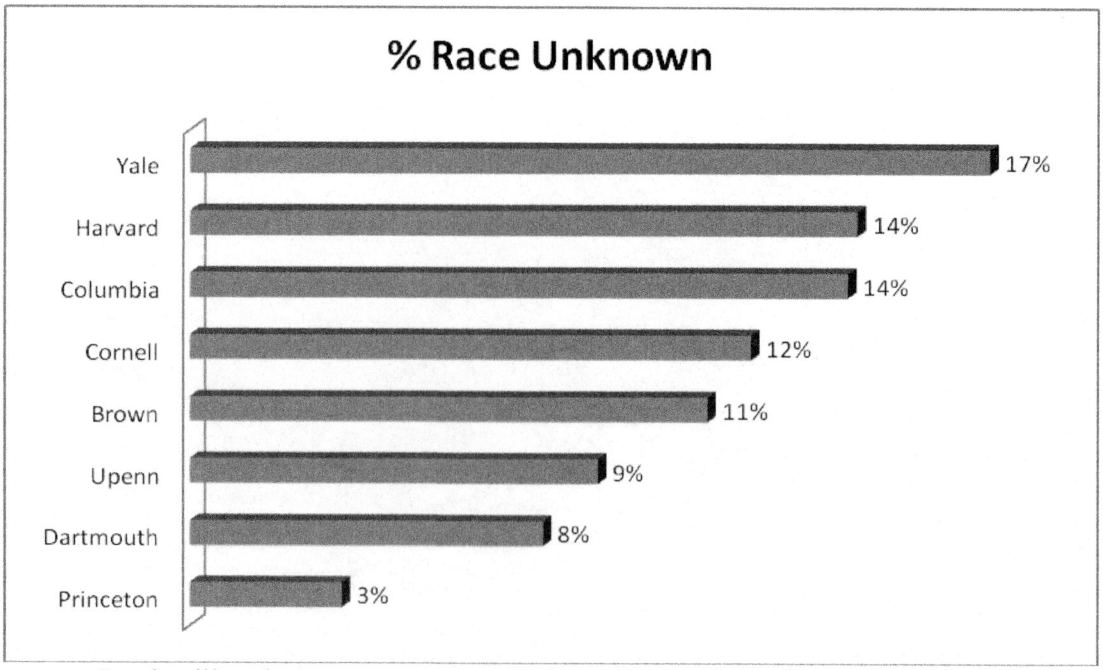

Looks like there are even more "race known" students in Yale. The caliber of students at Princeton, Yale and Harvard are largely viewed to be equal. So why the huge disparity in "race unknown" from Princeton (3%) to Yale (17%)? You can draw your own conclusions based on our analysis above. As lawyers, we can state that you do NOT need to provide your ethnicity if you do not wish to. And for particular schools, it would be an advantage to do so. Since we have specific suggestions for every school in this book, you are well-advised to review our "secrets" for a particular school.

Know Yourself and Your Opponent (School)

But how about those students that complains they receive rejections even though they even better numbers than the 75 percentile numbers? It's obvious that those students are not "attacking" the admission process the right way.

For example, Harvard boasts about 40 athletics teams, with 17% of the students participating. Each year, senior of those team graduate and coach need to fill their roster with competent replacements. And you (the student) can be that replacement, if you have some athletic skills. Please understand sports is **big in America**. Harvard and Yale have a huge rivalry, from football to track. Harvard does not want to be beaten in any sport by its arch rival in any sport. Same for Yale.

Specifically, we went to the athletic website of Harvard, (www.goCrimson.com) and review the rosters of the men's and women's track and field team for the 2010-11 season. Out of 111 team members listed, there are 4 Asian student-athletes. That comes out to only 3.6%. And each year, there are approximate 28 "openings (111/4) due to graduation. That represents some very nice "side door" opportunities.

We checked out another sport that is very popular with Asian students in high school – tennis. Out of the 22 members on the Harvard men's and women's tennis teams, 4 are Asian for the 2010-11 season. That would be an 18% representation. And other sports like football and lacrosse, there are practically no Asians.

Suffice to say that the Asian student-athlete percentage in Harvard is **much less** than the approximate 25% "real" population in Harvard. Consequently, the "athletic way" is a "secret" way to schools like Harvard. We are confident to say that using your athletic "hook," you would feel more welcome rather than rejected. Please see chart below.

<u>% Students who participate in Varsity Sports at College Level</u>

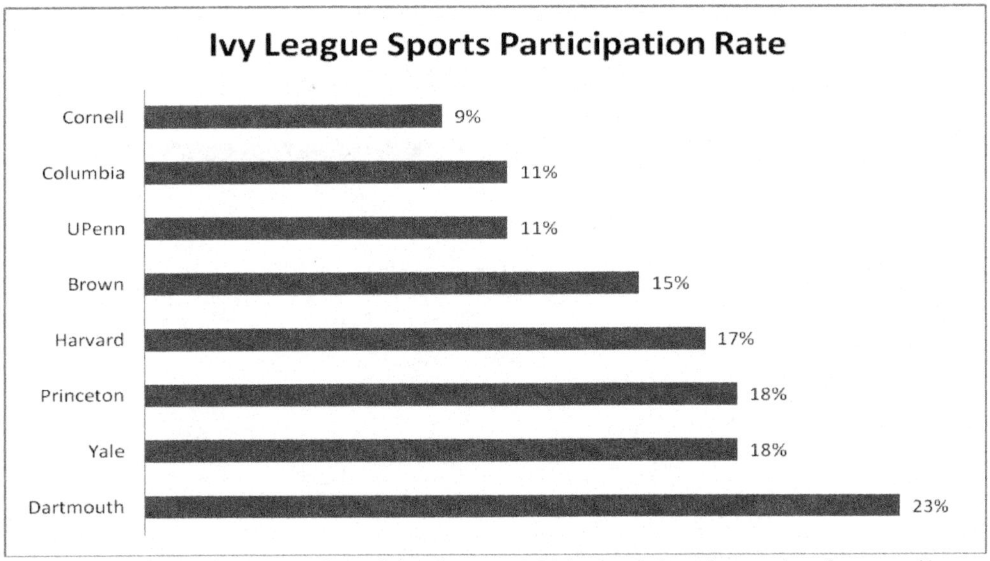

Take a look at Dartmouth, with almost 25% participation. As the smallest enrollment in the Ivy League, Dartmouth needs you (the student) to fill its athletic teams. So if you the student already has a 2,350 SAT, there is NO need to get that extra 50 points for a perfect SAT. Instead, practice improving your serve in tennis, or lowering your swim times (assuming you are a tennis player or swimmer).

So how good of an athlete do you have to be? Of course, a "national level" athlete would be a shoo-in. But if analyzed closely, many athletes in Harvard (regardless of ethnicity) are not "national level" athletes. We have special section in this book on the type of sports to participate as well as how good you need to be. And if you are still not sure, please feel free to contact us and we would be glad to analyze for you.

Applying the Correct Major

Another "secret" to increase your chances is to apply to schools where your major (not ethnicity) would be a minority. For example, an Asian student intending to study science or engineering would more likely to apply to schools such as MIT, Cal Tech and Stanford, than Harvard. Why? Because most think Harvard is a "liberal arts" school."

However, Harvard offers degrees in math and science. If students and parents look at the data we compiled, only 27% of undergraduates Harvard degrees conferred are in math, science or engineering. The rest 73% are in liberal arts. However, if you are a science major, you would be in "demand" in Harvard, or at least stand out in the application pile in Harvard, as compared to MIT.

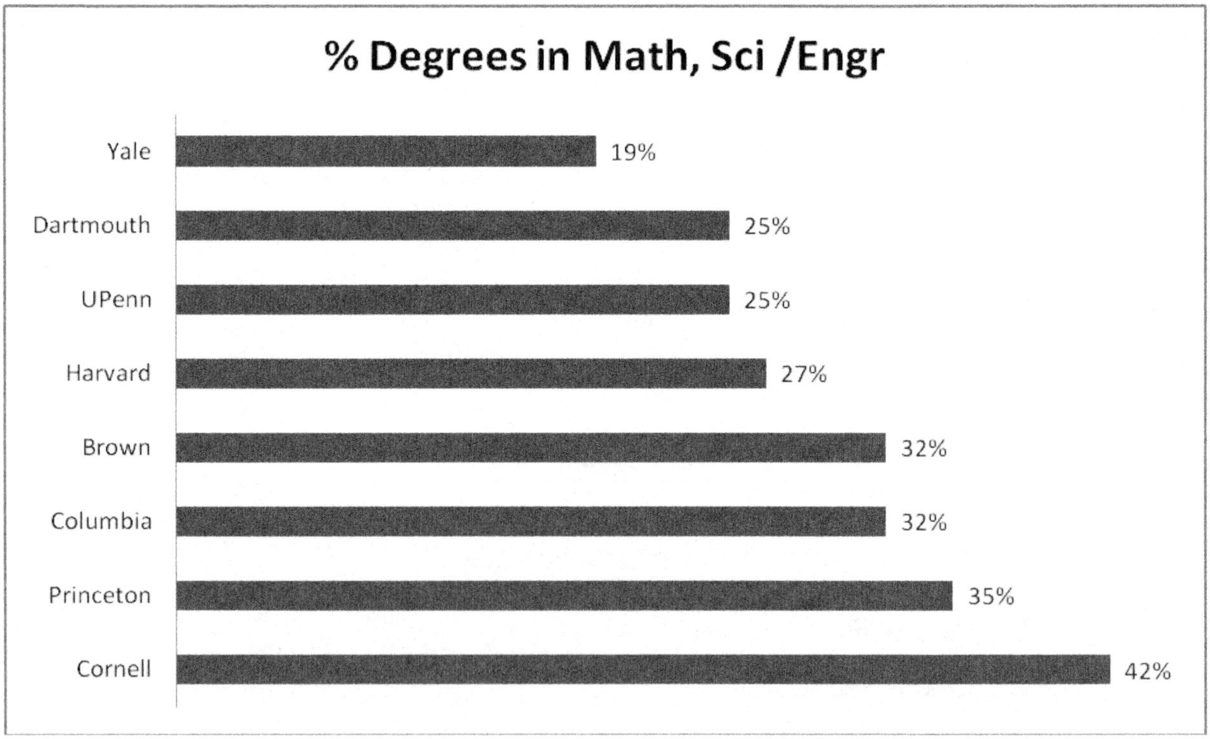

Most students only focus on test scores and GPA. But Harvard and the Ivy League take a "holistic" (overall) approach.

Summary

Thus, to recap, if you are an Asian student-athlete applying to Harvard and the Ivy League, your chance of admissions is already higher than the rest of the "Asian pile." Just by improving your athletic skills and your grades, you may be gain admission to the Ivy League school of your dreams (and that of your parents). We are profiling this Conference in this order:

Ivy League:

Harvard
Yale
Princeton
Brown
Columbia
Cornell
Dartmouth
UPenn

Harvard University

A) Ethnicity

White	Asian	Race Unknown	Int'l Students
44%	17%	14%	10%

B) Admission Rates

Overall Admit Rate	Regular Admit Rate	Early Action/ Early Decision
5.92%	4.2%	18.2%

C) Test Scores

SAT	**25 Percentile**	**75 Percentile**
Reading	690	800
Math	700	780
Writing	690	790
ACT	31	35

D) Financial Aid

% 1st Yr Student Receiving Grants	Avg Grants 1st Yr Student	Total Cost of Attendance (COA)
66%	$39,164	$55,050

E) Majors and Fields of Study

% Degrees in Math, Sci/Engr	Degrees in Other
27%	73%

Harvard University

Harvard – the dream school for students and parents from all over the world. Some parents even consulted *feng shui* consultants on how to get into Harvard. But why don't we just ask Harvard directly?

And Harvard does indeed respond, in the form of the "Common Data Set," the very cornerstone of data upon this book is written. First, Asian students who are strong in Computer Science ("CS") and Math should apply. Why? Because according to National Center of Education Statistics for Harvard, the percentage of students that graduate with bachelors in those 2 majors is low (Math = 5% and CS = 2%).

Use Leverage for Major

We understand that Harvard is not usually at the "top" of students and parents' ranking in computer science. Most students and parents think MIT, Stanford, or Cal Tech is better. We have two responses to such "closed-minded" thinking. First, Harvard is Harvard. And if that is not enough to convince you, then try this: Mark Zuckerberg, founder of Facebook studied Computer Science in Harvard (like Bill Gates, he dropped out before graduating). Then Zuckerberg went on to found Facebook and the rest is history.

As discussed in another section, Asian students need to take advantage of their strengths in math and study it in college. There is no need to keep chasing "hot" majors like biology or business. Indeed, 12% of Harvard bachelor degrees are awarded to bio-related majors. (Harvard has no undergraduate business major).

Ethnicity and Leverage

Chart A clearly shows Harvard already has 17% Asian (Ivy League avg. = 16.8%). Thus, Asian are already considered "over-represented" in Harvard. Furthermore, we believe a large portion of the 14% race "unknown" is Asian or white. Thus, Asians are even more overly represented. Thus, ethnicity by itself has absolutely no leverage.

Then we have to look at sports. With the most number of athletic teams of any college in the U.S. (according to Harvard), 17% of Harvard students play on its varsity teams. Thus, if Asian students can contribute their athletic skills, then their chances would increase drastically. Although Harvard's Asian population is 17%, Asian student-athletes do NOT make up 17% of Harvard's varsity teams. Thus, it can be concluded that Harvard is looking for Asian student-athletes. (Please also see our section on college sports).

Academics

If you are able to land a "lottery ticket" into Harvard, you can expect a great academic environment, but without too much pressure. It is widely known that Harvard has grade inflation. For example, in a recent graduating class, 70% of students graduated with honors. Thus, if you put in effort, you grades (mostly A's and A-'s) will reflect that.

With those grades, the Harvard name, and one of the strongest alumni network around the world, it is no wonder Harvard graduates make plenty of money, according to www.payscale.com, Harvard graduates can expect mid-career (15 years experience) salaries of $121K, which is just behind Princeton and Dartmouth. If you want a Ph.D., Harvard is the place to go. According to the National Science Foundation, Harvard ranks 11th in science/engineering Ph.D. rate (9.9%), above Yale's 8.4%.

Show Me the Money

With all these great features, we almost forgot to talk about money. Being the richest school in America, Harvard is more than generous. It showers 1st year students with an average of $39K in grants – highest in the Ivy League. Against the total Cost of Attendance (COA) of $55,050, that represents a huge 71% discount off the sticker price. A whopping 66% of first year students receive that amount of money. Harvard's 71% discount is also the largest in the Ivy, as it beats Yale (66%) and Princeton (68%). Thus, receiving admission into Harvard is a lottery ticket.

Conclusion:

In summary, the following "strategies" would increase your Harvard chances:

1) Apply for Early Action
2) Apply for math, computer science or physics major (4.5% students study those subjects);
3) Be a student-athlete;
4) For non-athletes: show depth and not breadth (i.e. show your passion or talent at a particular activity). Do not try to be "well rounded." Harvard is not looking for this type of students;
5) Race = unknown or international.

Yale University

A) Ethnicity

White	Asian	Race Unknown	Int'l Students
42%	14%	17%	9%

B) Admission Rates

Overall Admit Rate	Regular Admit Rate	Early Action/ Early Decision
6.82%	5.3%	15.7%

C) Test Scores

SAT	**25 Percentile**	**75 Percentile**
Reading	700	800
Math	700	780
Writing	700	790
ACT	30	34

D) Financial Aid

% 1st Yr Student Receiving Grants	Avg Grants 1st Yr Student	Total Cost of Attendance (COA)
58%	$36,668	$55,850

E) Majors and Fields of Study

% Degrees in Math, Sci/Engr	Degrees in Other
19%	81%

Yale and Harvard have a huge rivalry going back to the 19th century. If you attend Yale, you will learn to "hate" Harvard. Located in New Haven, Connecticut (2 hrs. from New York City; 2.5 hrs from Boston), Yale makes up the "Big Three" along with Harvard and Princeton. With undergrad at about 5,200 (same as Princeton), the male-female split is 50-50.

Residential College System

The name "Yale" conjures up image of East Coast elitism. But actually, it is place very students are mostly supportive of each other, like a family. Yale has a unique residential system, where each freshman is randomly assigned one of twelve "residential colleges." Each college has a dean and faculty members who live with students of that college. The students of a college eat and study together for the entire 4 years of their stay at Yale.

It is easy to see how networks can form and solidify under this system. Thus, it is not surprising that Yale's alumni network is one of the strongest in the world (not just in the U.S.). Students really don't need to worry about making friends or contacts – Yale's residential system takes care of that.

Financial Aid & Career Prospects

A strong alumni network ensures a strong Yale endowment for financial aid.
58% of Yale's 1st year students receive an average grant of $36,668 (Chart D). Against the total Cost of Attendance (COA) of $55,850, that represents a 66% discount off the sticker price. This 66% discount is one of the largest of any school profiled in this book. It only trails Harvard (71%) and Princeton (68%) in the Ivy League.

As for mid-career salary (15 years experience), Yale graduates report an excellent figure of $110K. This is according to www.payscale.com. This number, however falls a bit against Harvard ($121K), Princeton ($123K) and Stanford ($119K), but Yale does beat Brown ($109K) and UC-Berkeley ($109K).

According to the National Science Foundation, Yale is ranked 17th among all schools in the U.S. for science/engineer Ph.D. rate, which measures the likelihood of Ph.D.'s from a particular school. Yale's 8.4% rate is ranked right above Stanford (8.1%) and Cornell (7.6%), but below Harvard (9.9%) and Princeton (10.3%).

Thus, not only is Yale one of the best schools in the U.S., it is also clearly a generous school.

Ethnicity & Leverage?

That sounds great, so how can Asian students gain an advantage? Certainly not from an ethnicity basis, as Chart A shows Asian at 17%. However, we believe at least half of the 17% race "unknown" are Asian students. Thus, Asians at Yale would already be "over-represented."

So we turn out attention to sports. With as many teams as Harvard, 18% of Yale's students participate in inter-collegiate sports teams. If you can find a "place" on one of these teams, that could be your ticket into Yale. (Please also see our special section on particular sports). With a strong sport rivalry versus Harvard, Yale is always seeking student-athletes. Thus, your athletics skills will set you apart from the competition.

Study Science and Liberal Arts

Chart E shows that 19% of Yale students study math, science and engineering. For those majors, the most popular is Biology and related (7.5%), and then Engineering is 4%. Among liberal arts majors, Political Science (15%) and History (12.4%) lead the way. Furthermore, Math (2%) and Computer Science (1%) are some of the least popular majors at Yale.

Conclusion

In summary, the following road map will increase your chances at Yale:

1) Applying for Early Action (chances almost double the regular admission. Males even higher);
2) Apply for math, science or engineering (only 19% of student major in those subjects);
3) Student-athlete.

Princeton University

A) Ethnicity

White	Asian	Race Unknown	Int'l Students
48%	17%	3%	10%

B) Admission Rates

Overall Admit Rate	Regular Admit Rate	Early Action/ Early Decision
7.86%	5.9%	21.1%

C) Test Scores

SAT	25 Percentile	75 Percentile
Reading	690	790
Math	710	790
Writing	700	790
ACT	31	35

D) Financial Aid

% 1st Yr Student Receiving Grants	Avg Grants 1st Yr Student	Total Cost of Attendance (COA)
61%	$35,713	$52,670

E) Majors and Fields of Study

% Degrees in Math, Sci/Engr	Degrees in Other
35%	65%

Princeton University

Princeton was founded in 1746, before America was officially born. It seems that Harvard, Yale and Princeton take turns as the "top college" in the annual *U.S. News & World Report* rankings. Along with Stanford, students simply refer these 4 schools as "HYPS." Getting admitted into just one of these 4 schools is the dream of many students.

Financial Aid & Career Prospects

61% of Princeton's 1st year students receive an average grant of $35,713 (Chart D). Against the total Cost of Attendance (COA) of $52,670, that represents a big 68% discount off the sticker price. Princeton's 68% discount is only behind Harvard (71%) among Ivy League schools.

As for mid-career salary (15 years experience), Princeton is ranked 2d (tied with Dartmouth) with an amount of $123K, according to www.payscle.com. The $123K figure beats Harvard ($121K), Yale ($110K) and Stanford ($119K).

Princeton also ranks high in science/engineering Ph.D. rate, according to National Science Foundation. With 10th place ranking (10.3%), it ranks in front of Harvard (9.9%), Yale (8.4%) and Stanford (8.1%).

There is no doubt that Princeton is worthy of its top ranking and it is a generous school.

Ethnicity & Leverage

With a population of 17%, Asians cannot be described as "under-represented" (the Ivy League average is 15.8%). Thus, just like Harvard and Yale, we have to look for other ways to "climb" in.

Princeton has many athletics teams and 18% of its student body participate. We know for sure that there are not 18% Asian student-athletes in Princeton. Thus, the Asian student-athlete would have leverage. How good of an athlete? That depends on the sport. Princeton has national level lacrosse, fencing and basketball teams (men's). Other than those sports, Asian student-athletes should use their skills to their advantage. (Please also see our special section of particular sports).

Study Science and Liberal Arts

Why is Princeton consistently ranked so high? It may seem simple but professors focus on teaching undergraduates. At Princeton, students can expect small classes. In fact, only 9% of all Princeton classes exceed 30 students (the lowest in the Ivy League). Put another way, 91% of Princeton classes have 30 students or less. No UC or another public school comes close to this figure.

Chart E also shows that many students in Princeton study math, science and engineering (35%). Engineering is actually the single most popular major in Princeton (19%), while Biology is at 8%. Among liberal art majors, Political Science (9%) and Economics (8%) are the front runners.

Conclusion:

In summary, the following attributes will increase your chance at Princeton:

1) Applying for Math majors (2.6% of graduates);
2) Princeton currently has no Early Decision or Early Action, but has announced that it would implement an Early Action program for HS Class of 2013-Apply for Early Action, if possible;
3) Student-athlete (18% participation among students, 2d highest in Ivy League);
4) Race unknown.

Brown University

A) Ethnicity

White	Asian	Race Unknown	Int'l Students
46%	15%	11%	10%

B) Admission Rates

Overall Admit Rate	Regular Admit Rate	Early Action/ Early Decision
9.6%	8.5%	19.0%

C) Test Scores

SAT	**25 Percentile**	**75 Percentile**
Reading	660	760
Math	670	770
Writing	670	770
ACT	29	33

D) Financial Aid

% 1st Yr Student Receiving Grants	Avg Grants 1st Yr Student	Total Cost of Attendance (COA)
49%	$34,611	$54,370

E) Majors and Fields of Study

% Degrees in Math, Sci/Engr	Degrees in Other
30%	70%

Brown University

Located in Providence, Rhode Island (1 hr. from Boston), Brown is ranked 15th (tied with Cornell) in the latest *U.S. News* rankings. With an undergrad enrollment of approximately 6,300, Brown also has the largest gender gap in the Ivy League (53% female vs. 47% male).

No Major Requirements

Brown's unique academic experience allows students to design their own majors. With no requirements, Brown students are encouraged to explore different subjects. Many courses can be taken on pass/fail basis. In some ways, Brown students face the least amount of academic pressure in the Ivy League.

Many Asian parents do not feel comfortable with this "lack of requirement approach." They often do not think that 18 year-old can effectively design a plan of study. We, however, feel that Brown's approach is effective because it develops students thinking skills, a critical skill in today's fast moving world.

At Brown, "no requirements" and liberal pass/fail policies allows science/math majors to venture into liberal arts classes and develop their critical thinking skills. It is doubtful that such a student would take Contemporary Buddhism (for example) at a UC school. In recent years, Brown is known for attracting celebrities such as Emma Watson (Harry Potter movies), which in turn increases Brown's status even more among applicants.

Financial Aid & Career Prospects

49% of Brown's 1st year students receive an average grant of $34,611 (Chart D). Against the total Cost of Attendance (COA) of $54,370, that represents a substantial 64% discount off the sticker price. Brown's 64% discount at the average of the Ivy League schools (63%).

As for mid-career salary (15 years experience), Brown graduates report an average of $109K, according to www.payscle.com. This is an outstanding figure as Brown beats several schools ranked ahead of them. Specifically, Brown beats Univ. of Chicago (9th/$100K), Northwestern (12th/$91.9K) and Washington Univ. St-Louis (13th/$91.4K). Looks like Brown's "no requirement" curriculum also results in high salary.

Brown also ranks high in science/engineering Ph.D. rate, according to National Science Foundation. With 25th place ranking (7.4%), Brown ranks in front of Dartmouth (5.7%), but behind Cornell (7.6%) and Johns Hopkins (7.7%). Against other schools ranked close to it, Brown's Ph. D rate overwhelms schools such as Northwestern (not ranked) and Washington Univ. St-Louis (not ranked).

One of these successful Brown graduates who later obtained a Ph.D. is Dr. Jim Yong Kim, the President of Dartmouth. Dr. Kim is currently the first and only Asian to be president of an Ivy League school.

Based on the above factors, Brown is an excellent school that is also generous. Actually, we think so highly of Brown that we believe that it is the most underrated school in the top-20 of *U.S. News* rankings (Please see our special section on overrated vs. underrated schools).

Ethnicity & Leverage

Chart A shows that's Whites outnumber Asians by 3-to-1 (46% vs. 15%) at Brown. This shows that Asians are not under-represented, especially when factoring in the 11% "race unknown." Thus, we need to look at leverage again.

Sports could provide Asian applicant with a boost. Traditionally, Brown sports team are not as strong as the Big Three. Furthermore, with a student participation rate of 15%, there are plenty of opportunities for Asian student-athletes to step up. (Please also see our special section on particular sports). As we mentioned in other sections, athletics can push your application "in."

Study Science and Liberal Arts

Chart E shows that plenty of Brown students (30%) study math, science and engineering (yes, Brown has Engr. Majors). For those majors, the most popular is Biology and related (16%), and then Engineering is at 6%. Among liberal arts majors, Economics (8%) and English (5.5%) are the favorites.

Conclusion:

So here are the "secrets" of getting into Brown for Asian students:

1) Apply for Early Decision (more than twice as likely as Regular Admission);
2) A student-athlete (see discussion above);
3) Male (Brown has 53% female);
4) Declare your science/math major immediately and you will stand out;
5) From the West or South.

Columbia University

A) Ethnicity

White	Asian	Race Unknown	Int'l Students
40%	15%	14%	10%

B) Admission Rates

Overall Admit Rate	Regular Admit Rate	Early Action/Early Decision
7.42%	6.02%	20.4%

C) Test Scores

SAT	**25 Percentile**	**75 Percentile**
Reading	680	780
Math	690	780
Writing	680	770
ACT	31	34

D) Financial Aid

% 1st Yr Student Receiving Grants	Avg Grants 1st Yr Student	Total Cost of Attendance (COA)
47%	$32,915	$61,460

E) Majors and Fields of Study

% Degrees in Math, Sci/Engr	Degrees in Other
32%	68%

Columbia University

Situated in the "City that Never Sleeps" (New York), Columbia is so "hot" among applicants that its admission rate is now 6.4%, which is very close to Harvard's 6.2%. Put another way, they reject almost 94 out of every 100 applicants. Ranked *No. 4* in the latest *U.S. News* rankings, Columbia has about 7,700 undergrads with an even male-female split. Just like Ivy peers Cornell and UPenn, students must apply to a particular school in Columbia. A ticket to Columbia could be an exciting 4 years of studying and internship experiences, and plenty of job options after graduation.

Financial Aid & Career Prospects

47% of Columbia's 1st year students receive an average grant of $32,915 (Chart D). Against the total Cost of Attendance (COA) of $61,466, that represents a 54% discount off the sticker price. Columbia's 54% discount is the lowest in the Ivy League, and well below the Ivy average of 63%.

As for mid-career salary (15 years experience), Columbia graduates report an average of $99.7K, according to www.payscle.com. For a school ranked so high (4th), Columbia's salary number is the lowest in the Ivy League. Furthermore, Columbia salary number also fails to beat schools ranked nearby. Specifically, Columbia's salary number cannot match Harvard (1st/$121K), Princeton (2nd/$123K), Yale (3rd/$123K), UPenn (5th/$111K), Stanford (5th/$119K), and MIT (7th/$119K).

Furthermore, Columbia's salary number place it near schools ranked lower, such as Rice (17th/$100K), USC (23rd/$99.7K) and Cal-Poly San Luis Obispo ($99.2K). For Ph. D. rate, Columbia (along with UPenn) is not ranked in the top-50 schools whose graduates obtain Ph.D. later on. This is according to National Science Foundation. This fact is shocking since 17% of Columbia students study engineering, much higher percentage than liberal art schools that are ranked by the Nat'l Science Foundation.

Overall, the mid-career salary is low compare to other elite schools. Also, Columbia's discount for financial aid is the lowest in the Ivy League. Thus, we conclude that Columbia is not that generous. And considering its low admit rate, students should apply to other more generous schools as well.

Ethnicity & Leverage?

Again, Columbia has an all-time low admit rate of 6.4% (Chart B). Chart A shows that Columbia has already 15% Asians. This "actual" percentage will most likely be higher since there are also 14% "race unknown," many of whom are believed to be Asian. Thus, what kind of leverage would help an Asian applicant?

The simple answer is sports. Only 11% of Columbia students participate in their varsity teams, thus leaving plenty of opportunities for willing participants. We theorize this low participation rate because there are just too many activities to do in New York City. Furthermore, Columbia's teams traditionally has been the weakest in the Ivy. (Please also see our special section on particular sports). Thus, Asian student-athlete would have leverage.

Study Science and Liberal Arts

Chart E shows that 32% of Columbia students study math, science and engineering. For those majors, the most popular is Engineering (17%) and Biology (6%). Among liberal arts majors, Economics (10.5%), History (7%) and English (7%) are the favorites.

Conclusion

So here are the strategies for increasing your chances to Columbia:

1) Apply for Early Decision (more than twice as likely as Regular Admission);
2) Ethnicity = Unknown;
3) A student-athlete;
4) Geographic diversity (CA students have a slight edge over NY students).

Cornell University

A) Ethnicity

White	Asian	Race Unknown	Int'l Students
46%	16%	12%	9%

B) Admission Rates

Overall Admit Rate	Regular Admit Rate	Early Action/Early Decision
16.2%	14.5%	32.5%

C) Test Scores

SAT	**25 Percentile**	**75 Percentile**
Reading	640	730
Math	670	770
Writing	660	760
ACT	30	34

D) Financial Aid

% 1st Yr Student Receiving Grants	Avg Grants 1st Yr Student	Total Cost of Attendance (COA)
51%	$33,653	$57,285

E) Majors and Fields of Study

% Degrees in Math, Sci/Engr	Degrees in Other
42%	58%

Cornell University

Ranked 15th in the latest *U.S. News* rankings, Cornell is located in scenic Ithaca, NY (1 hr from Syracuse and 5 hrs from New York City). Although its reputation is in science and engineering (42%/Chart D), Cornell offers perhaps the most courses and majors in the Ivy League. Just like Ivy peers UPenn and Columbia, a student must apply to a specific school for admission. With the largest undergrad enrollment in the Ivy League (almost 14,000), Cornell has a 50-50 male/female split.

Financial Aid & Career Prospects

49% of Cornell's 1st year students receive an average grant of $33,653 (Chart D). Against the total Cost of Attendance (COA) of $57,285, that represents a nice 59% discount off the sticker price. Cornell's 59% discount beats schools ranked nearby, specifically Northwestern (12th/48%), Johns Hopkins (13th/53%), Wash. Univ.-St. Louis (13th/41%), but falls behind Brown (15th/64%).

As for mid-career salary (15 years experience), Cornell graduates report a robust figure of $106K. This is according to www.payscale.com. Again, Cornell's salary figures beats several schools ranked ahead of them. Specifically, Cornell beats Univ. of Chicago ($100K), Northwestern ($91.9K), Wash. Univ.-St. Louis ($91.4K) but falls short vs. Brown ($109K).

According to the National Science Foundation, Cornell is ranked 22nd among all schools in the U.S. for science/engineer Ph.D. rate, which measures the likelihood of Ph.D.'s from a particular school. Cornell's 7.6% rate is ranked right below Stanford (8.1%) and Hopkins (7.7%), and just above Brown (7.4%). Actually, 6 of out 8 Ivy League schools are ranked in the top-50 for Ph.D. rate (except for Columbia and UPenn).

Overall, with a nice discount, robust mid-career salary number, and high Ph.D. rate, we conclude Cornell is a generous school.

Ethnicity & Leverage?

Chart A shows that Whites outnumber Asians by almost 3-to-1 (46% vs. 16%). Furthermore, 12% Cornell students are "race unknown." It is our belief that most of the race "unknown" students are actually White and/or Asian. Thus, Asian "ethnicity" by itself is not enough of leverage.

However, geography can be used as "leverage" as Cornell seeks to recruits students from West and South. Sports is also another "leverage." For student-athletes, you do not need to be "national level" unless you are in men's **ice hockey or** men's **lacrosse**, two sports that Cornell is a perennial power. In sports other than those two, students-athletes just need to be "good" to "very good" (please also see our special section on particular sports).

Study Science/Engineering and Liberal Arts

Chart E shows that 42% of Cornell students study math, science and engineering (highest in the Ivy League). Indeed, the most popular major overall is engineering (18%). Of course, Biology and bio-medical science cannot be too far behind (12%). Moreover, plenty of students study other majors (58%) such as liberal arts, Architecture, Business, Nutrition Science and Agricultural Economics. Among those, Business (13%) Economics (11%), and Architecture (5%) lead the way.

Get admitted to Cornell's A&S as a liberal arts major, and *life can be good.* It's hard to get in but **easy** to go through. You will work (but not too hard) and be rewarded with at around 3.5 GPA, which sets you up for top PH.D. programs or law schools. (See Ph. D. rate discussion above). A **hidden gem** in the Ivy League, Cornell's Arts & Science School has a <u>small enrollment</u> so you will receive lots of personal attention (& high grades). Thus, students can double-major and/or "Study Abroad" to enrich their experience.

Conclusion:

Here are the attributes for a successful applicant to Cornell (Co-author Allen Leung is a Cornell alum):

1) Females apply for Engr.; Males apply for Liberal Arts
2) From Midwest or West Coast;
3) Student-Athlete;
4) Apply Early Decision (almost double chance of Regular Decision);
5) Ethnicity= International or "Unknown";
6) Essay = Show "Fit".

Dartmouth College

A) Ethnicity

White	Asian	Race Unknown	Int'l Students
49%	14%	8%	8%

B) Admission Rates

Overall Admit Rate	Regular Admit Rate	Early Action/ Early Decision
9.4%	8.0%	25.8%

C Test Scores

SAT	**25 Percentile**	**75 Percentile**
Reading	670	780
Math	690	790
Writing	690	790
ACT	30	34

D) Financial Aid

% 1st Yr Student Receiving Grants	Avg Grants 1st Yr Student	Total Cost of Attendance (COA)
47%	$37,022	$58,683

E) Majors and Fields of Study

% Degrees in Math, Sci/Engr	Degrees in Other
25%	75%

Dartmouth College

As the only "college" in the Ivy League and with the smallest enrollment, Dartmouth focuses on undergraduate students. Dartmouth (ranked 9th in latest *U.S. News* rankings) is located in Hanover, New Hampshire (2.3 hrs from Boston).

Dartmouth D-Plan

Dartmouth operates on a trimester schedule with a unique feature (commonly refer to as the "D-Plan"). The D-Plan allows students plenty of time and opportunities to explore their interest through internships and study abroad. The unique feature of the D-Plan is that all students must spend the summer after their sophomore year at Dartmouth to get to know their classmates.

Thus, a student can study in France in the fall of the sophomore year. Then s/he can work in New York for 2 months, and then head to China for the spring semester for study/internship. Then s/he will be back on campus for the summer to tell friends about such experience. That is the quintessential D-Plan experience. An example is Timothy Geithner, the current U.S. Secretary of Treasury (Finance Minister), who studied abroad in China while he was a student at Dartmouth.

Financial Aid & Career Prospects

47% of Dartmouth's 1st year students receive an average grant of $37,022 (Chart D). Against the total Cost of Attendance (COA) of $58,638, that represents a 63% discount off the sticker price. This 63% discount matches the Ivy League average.

As for mid-career salary (15 years experience), Dartmouth is No. 2 among all schools in the U.S. With a figure of $123K, Dartmouth is tied with Princeton, besting other schools from the Ivy League. (Harvey Mudd from California is the champion at $126K). Yes, even Yale ($110K), Harvard ($121K) and Stanford ($119K) cannot match Dartmouth's salary number.

According to the National Science Foundation, Dartmouth is ranked 40th among all schools in the U.S. for science/engineer Ph.D. rate, which measures the likelihood of Ph.D.'s from a particular school. Dartmouth 5.7% rate is tied with UC-Berkeley but below other Harvard, Yale and Princeton.

Our impression is that many Asian parents generally dismissed Dartmouth as a "high priority" school on their kids' application list. Most Asian parents' view of the Ivy League is this: either the "Big Three" (Harvard/Yale/Princeton), or nothing. Well, we like those parents to consider the fact that Dartmouth also throws in an average of $37K in grants for qualified freshman (47%). All of the above factors lead to the conclusion that Dartmouth is a wonderful and generous school.

Ethnicity & Leverage?

Chart A shows that there are 14% Asians in Dartmouth, the lowest in the Ivy League. Dartmouth is clearly committed to seek high-achieving Asian students. This is evidenced by naming Dr. Jim Yong Kim as its President in 2009. Dr. Kim is the first Asian to lead an Ivy League school.

The leverage for Asian students is same for all Ivy schools – sports. Dartmouth actually has the highest percentage of students who play college sports (23%) among Ivy League schools. (Please also see our special section on particular sports.) Thus, Dartmouth really needs student-athletes. If you can play a sport reasonably well, your chances would be much greater than the ones shown on Chart B.

The next leverage on the list would be choice of major. Again, not enough Asian students major in math and physical sciences. Thus, these majors allows interested students an easier way into Dartmouth.

Study Science and Liberal Arts

Chart E shows that 25% of Dartmouth students study math, science and engineering. For those majors, the most popular is Biology and related (10.5%), and then Engineering is at 5%. Among liberal arts majors, Economics (14%) and History (7%) are the favorites.

Parents and students should not discount the value of Dartmouth's liberal arts education, which is studied by 75 % of its students (Chart E). Dartmouth alumni network is one of the strongest in Wall St., that has allowed its graduates salary to flourish (see salary discussion above). And no, Dartmouth, do <u>not</u> have undergraduate majors in business.

Conclusion

In summary, based upon the data, you would be a successful candidate for admission into Dartmouth if:

1) Apply for Early Decision;
2) Student-athlete (23% of Dartmouth students play on its varsity teams);
3) Apply for math or science major (only 25% of Dartmouth degrees);
4) Asians account for only 14% in Dartmouth, **<u>lowest</u>** of the Ivy League.

University of Pennsylvania

A) Ethnicity

White	Asian	Race Unknown	Int'l Students
46%	19%	9%	11%

B) Admission Rates

Overall Admit Rate	Regular Admit Rate	Early Action/ Early Decision
12.3%	10.1%	25.4%

C) Test Scores

SAT	**25 Percentile**	**75 Percentile**
Reading	660	750
Math	690	780
Writing	680	770
ACT	30	34

D) Financial Aid

% 1st Yr Student Receiving Grants	Avg Grants 1st Yr Student	Total Cost of Attendance (COA)
46%	$33,340	$57,366

E) Majors & Fields of Study

% Degrees in Math, Sci/Engr	Degrees in Other
25%	75%

University of Pennsylvania ("UPenn")

Founded by Benjamin Franklin 270 years ago in Philadelphia, UPenn has grown into a top research university with 20,000 graduates and undergraduates. Ranked 5th (tied with Stanford) in the latest *U.S. News* rankings, UPenn is perhaps most famous for its Wharton School of business (undergrad and MBA). UPenn has slightly more females (51%) than males (49%).

Financial Aid & Career Prospects

46% of UPenn's 1st year students receive an average grant of $33,460 (Chart D). Against the total Cost of Attendance (COA) of $57,366, that represents a 58% discount off the sticker price. UPenn's 58% discount, while substantial, falls short of the Ivy League average of 63%.

As for mid-career salary (15 years experience), UPenn graduates report a high average of $111K, according to www.payscle.com. This indeed is an outstanding number as it beats Yale ($100K), Brown ($109K), but falls short against Stanford ($119K) and Harvard ($121K).

Surprisingly, UPenn is not ranked in the top-50 schools for science and engineering Ph.D. rate, in a ranking release by the National Science Foundation. (Columbia and UPenn are the only 2 Ivy schools not on the list). The National Science Foundation measures the likelihood of graduates from particular school and determines whether they would obtain science and engineering Ph.D.'s later.

Despite this, we still conclude UPenn is a generous school due to the high mid-career salary and robust 58% discount to qualified students.

Ethnicity & Leverage

Chart B shows that UPenn has an admit rate of only 12.3% (all-time low). Chart A shows that UPenn has already 19% Asians. This actual percentage will probably be higher since there are also 9% "race unknown," many of whom are believed to be Asian. Thus, what kind of leverage would help an Asian applicant?

Perhaps we need to hear from the Dean of UPenn's admission himself. Eric Furda, UPenn's Dean of Admissions, actually gave some clues. He stated to the Daily Pennsylvanian (school newspaper) that physics and math majors at his school are "under-enrolled" (i.e. not enough students). Thus, if UPenn's Dean of Admission is stating he would like to see more students in UPenn studying Math and Physics. So what are you (math and physics majors) waiting for?

Students are instructed to listen to teachers in schools. Applicants to UPenn should listen and follow the advice from its Dean of Admission. The data from Chart E supports this strategy. As seen from Chart E, only 25% of UPenn students study math, science and engineering. UPenn's 25% is *less* than the percentage at Brown (30%), which has no requirements and a reputation as a pure liberal arts school. In any event, the road map to UPenn is math and science majors.

Athletics Any Help?

As we discussed in other parts of this book, Asian student-athletes are in short supply. Thus, sports can be used as leverage into the Ivy League and other highly competitive schools. (Please see our special section on particular sports). We reiterate that sports is perhaps the biggest leverage for Asian-American applicants.

Study Science and Liberal Arts

In addition to Wharton, UPenn has excellent programs in Engineering, Nursing, liberal arts and sciences. Moreover, UPenn's 25% of students in science/engineering (Chart E) make it resemble a liberal arts school, such as Dartmouth (25%) and Yale (19%).

For UPenn, 11% study Engineering and 10% study Biology. Dean Furda is right: UPenn is short on Math majors (1.5%) and Physics (1%). Among non-science/engineering majors, Business (14%) and Economics (6%) lead the way.

Conclusion:

In summary, the following strategies will increase your chances at UPenn:

1) Apply for Math, Physics or Computer Science majors (total only 3% of students);
2) Apply for Early Decision (chance for admission almost 3 times higher than Regular admissions);
3) Avoid applying to the ultra-competitive Wharton School;
4) Student-athlete

CONFERENCE TWO: Little Ivies/NESCAC Schools

In this section, we are profiling the schools nicknamed "Little Ivies" and other schools who are part of the New England Small College Athletic Conference ("NESCAC"). Although Swarthmore is not part of the NESCAC, we are profiling it as well due to its high ranking by *U.S. News* (4th in Liberal Arts).

These schools are also some of the most generous in America, much more generous than UC schools. Please see Chart below:

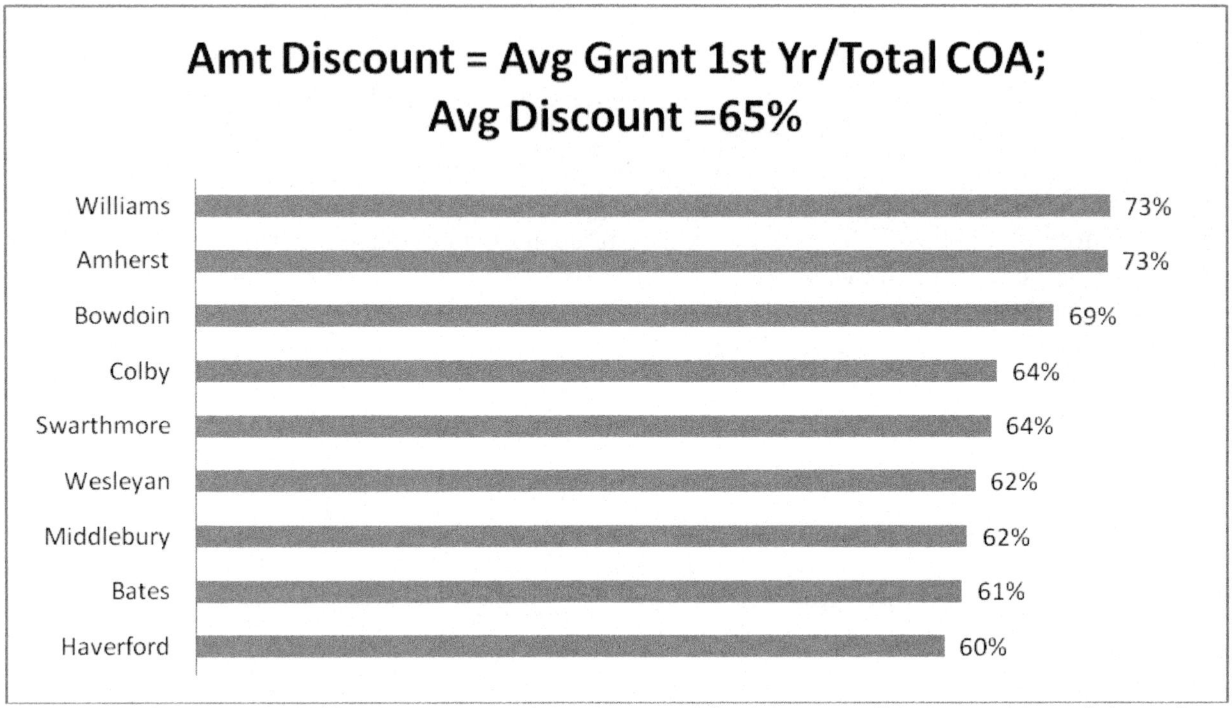

Amherst and Williams, not surprisingly, provide the most discounts. Bowdoin, a lesser-known school among Asian parents and students, has a discount of *almost 70%.* Again, we are advising parents and student don't just look at the "sticker" price of these schools. You need to look at the net price, or "out-the-door" price. You will also find that in addition to generous, these schools are excellent academically. We are profiling this Conference in the following order:

Little Ivies/NESCAC Schools:

Williams
Amherst
Wesleyan
Bates
Bowdoin
Colby
Middlebury
Haverford
Swarthmore

Williams College

A) Ethnicity

White	Asian	Race Unknown	Int'l Students
59%	10%	0%	7%

B) Admission Rates

Overall Admit Rate	Regular Admit Rate	Early Action/Early Decision
16.7%	14.5%	42.2%

C) Test Scores

SAT	**25 Percentile**	**75 Percentile**
Reading	680	770
Math	650	760
Writing	N/A	N/A
ACT	29	34

D) Financial Aid

% 1st Yr Student Receiving Grants	Avg Grants 1st Yr Student	Total Cost of Attendance (COA)
53%	$40,146	$55,032

E) Majors and Fields of Study

% Degrees in Math, Sci/Engr	Degrees in Other
27%	73%

Whereas Harvard, Yale and Princeton are known as the "Big Three" in the Ivy League, Amherst, Wesleyan and Williams are known as the "Little Three." But they are only "little" in terms of student enrollment. The "Little Three" has been consistently ranked as the top liberal arts schools in the U.S. Thus, the "Little Three" is on par with the "Big Three" and the Ivy league in many ways.

Located in Williamstown, western Massachusetts (3 hrs from Boston; 1 hr from Albany, NY), Williams is the classical Northeast liberal arts college. With a total student body of 2,000 (all undergrads), it boast a low student-to-faculty ratio of only 7 to 1. Furthermore, **37%** of Williams classes have 9 or less students (as a comparison, Harvard's percentage = 39% for such classes). Now, we can all see why Williams is part of the "Little Three."

Generous with Money?

Williams is anything but "little" when it comes to financial aid. Please see Chart D. As you can see, Williams grants $40K to qualified recipients (53% all 1st-Year students). Against a total COA of $55K, that is a whopping **73% discount** of the total cost (Harvard's "discount" to qualified students was 71%. Please see the Harvard section). Put another way, the "out-the-door" price is only **$15,000** ($55,000 - $40,000), before student loans and/or federal work-study, which could decrease your payments even further. If you receive such an award from Williams (assuming you get in of course), and you are comparing Williams vs. an UC school, we believe you should take the Williams offer.

Need more proof? According to Payscale.com, Williams graduates' mid-career salary of $106K beats all UC Schools except UC-Berkeley. Furthermore, Williams also beats Columbia (6.4% admission rate), whose amount is $99,700

Ethnicity

As shown on Chart A above, Asians has a 10% representation at Williams. It is the authors' opinion that this number is "borderline" underrepresentation. That means Asian applicants will have a "boost," assuming their GPA and test scores are great (i.e. 75th percentile of number in Charts C above). Unlike other liberal arts colleges, Williams is much more well-known among Asian students and parents. Thus, it is recommended that students apply Early Decision, where the chance are double that of the Regular cycle.

Athletics

Almost half (48%) of Williams students participate in its 30 inter-collegiate teams (more than many UC Schools). Thus, it is clear that Williams needs student-athletes to fill its team rosters. How good of an athlete do you need to be to have an edge in admissions? Traditionally, Williams is the strongest athletic team among the "Little Three." However, many students go study-abroad or quit the sports team after one year, thereby creating many openings on sports teams. Thus, if you have above average athletic skills in certain sports AND you state your willingness to participate once admitted to Williams, you chance of admission (and obtaining generous financial aid) could become "probable" from "maybe."

Not Just "Arts"

As shown on chart E above, plenty of Williams students study math and science (27%). The smaller classes (7-to-1 student to faculty ratio) allows for better learning in math and sciences. Bio-related majors (12%) is the most popular major among math/science majors. Moreover, 8.7% of Williams graduates goes on to obtain a science or engineering PH.Ds. That number is higher than Stanford's (8.1%).

Conclusion

In summary, the following "strategies" will increase your chances at Williams:

1) Apply for Early Decision (chances are more than double vs. Regular Admission);
2) Student-athletes (48% of Williams students play on its varsity teams);
3) Apply for math and science major (only 27% such students at Williams);
4) Ethnicity = Asian or International.

Amherst College

A) Ethnicity

White	Asian	Race Unknown	Int'l Students
39%	10%	13%	9%

B) Admission Rates

Overall Admit Rate	Regular Admit Rate	Early Action/Early Decision
11.9%	10%	NA

C) Test Scores

SAT	**25 Percentile**	**75 Percentile**
Reading	670	770
Math	670	770
Writing	680	770
ACT	30	34

D) Financial Aid

% 1st Yr Student Receiving Grants	Avg Grants 1st Yr Student	Total Cost of Attendance (COA)
54%	$39,962	$54,922

E) Majors and Fields of Study

% Degrees in Math, Sci/Engr	Degrees in Other
17%	83%

Amherst College

Like Williams, Amherst is located in a town that is named after the college: Amherst, Massachusetts (2 hrs from Boston; 60 miles Williams College). It is the "same" in many ways as Williams in many ways. Amherst's total enrollment is 1,800 and student-to-faculty ratio is 10-to-1. Amherst and Williams are probably the two most famous colleges among Asian students and parents. As we explained in other sections of this book, a liberal arts college can provide great financial aid and lay the foundation for even better career prospects. Realizing the above factors, students of all ethnicities have increased their applications to the "Little Three," leading to a frenzy that drops the admissions rate even lower. Let's see how students can gain an edge in admissions and financial aid.

Money Matters

Not to outdone by Williams, Amherst also provide a 73% discount to qualified 1st year students. Please see Chart D. Specifically, half of Amherst' first students receives an average of $39,962 in grants (not loans). When we factor in the total COA (Cost of Attendance) of $54,922, that comes out to a **73% discount** off the sticker price. That is very generous.

Need more proof? According to www.Payscale.com, Williams graduates' mid-career salary of $102K beats all UC Schools except UC-Berkeley. Furthermore, Williams' salary number also beats USC ($99,400).

Furthermore, according to the National Science Foundation, 6.8% Amherst grads go to obtain science and engineering PH.D's. That percentage is **higher** than UC-Berkeley (5.7%).

Ethnicity

As shown on Chart A above, Asians has a 10% representation at Williams. It is the authors' opinion that this number is "borderline" underrepresentation. That means Asian applicants will have a "boost," assuming their GPA and test scores are great (i.e. 75th percentile of number in Charts C above). Like Williams, Amherst is much more well-known among Asian students and parents. Thus, it is recommended that students apply Early Decision, where the chance are double that of the Regular cycle (especially for females).

Athletics

Thirty-seven percent of Amherst students participate in its inter-collegiate teams. Thus, it is clear that Amherst needs student-athletes to fill its team rosters and compete against other school, especially its arch-rival Williams. How good of an athlete do you need to be to have an edge in admissions? Traditionally, Williams' sports teams are usually very strong among liberal arts schools in the East, not just among the Big Three. Thus, Amherst feels a need to "keep up."

Moreover, many students go study-abroad or quit the sports team after one year, thereby creating many openings on sports teams. Thus, if you have above average athletic skills in certain sports AND you state your willingness to participate once admitted to Amherst, your chance of admission (and obtaining generous financial aid) just went up. Specifically, your chance as a student-athlete would be much higher than those listed in Chart A.

You Can Study Science as well as Liberal Arts

As shown on chart E above, plenty of Amherst students study math and science (18%). The smaller classes (8-to-1 student to faculty ratio) allows for better learning in math and sciences. Bio-related majors (7%) is the most popular major among math/science majors. Again, you can study science at a small school such as Amherst and still attend medical school (graduate school) later.

Conclusion

In summary, the following "strategies" will increase your chances at Amherst:

1) Apply for Early Decision, especially for females (chances are more than double vs. Regular Admission);
2) Student-athletes (37% of Amherst students play on its varsity teams);
3) Apply for math and science major (only 18% such students at Amherst);
4) Ethnicity = Asian or International

Wesleyan University

A) Ethnicity

White	Asian	Race Unknown	Int'l Students
56%	7%	9%	7%

B) Admission Rates

Overall Admit Rate	Regular Admit Rate	Early Action/Early Decision
19.7%	17.6%	44.5%

C) Test Scores

SAT	**25 Percentile**	**75 Percentile**
Reading	670	780
Math	680	760
Writing	680	780
ACT	30	34

D) Financial Aid

% 1st Yr Student Receiving Grants	Avg Grants 1st Yr Student	Total Cost of Attendance (COA)
47%	$34,728	$55,736

E) Majors and Fields of Study

% Degrees in Math, Sci/Engr	Degrees in Other
17%	83%

Wesleyan is the only school out of the "Little Three" that is an university. It is located in Middletown, Connecticut (30 miles from Yale; 100 miles from Brown, and 2 hours from New York City). It is also not as well-known as Amherst or Williams among Asian students and parents. But like these other 2 schools, Wesleyan is a liberal arts and "science" school.

Money Matters

Wesleyan offers a **62% discount** to qualified first-year students. And 47% of Wesleyan's freshmen students receive the discount ($34,728 vs. total COA of $55,736). That amount of generosity should grab your immediate attention if you have not heard much about Wesleyan.

Furthermore, according to the National Science Foundation, 7.1% Wesleyan grads go on to obtain science and engineering PH.D's. That percentage is right behind Brown (7.5%), but **higher** than UC-Berkeley (5.7%) or Amherst (6.8%).

Ethnicity

As shown on Chart A above, Asians has a 7% representation at Wesleyan, which in our opinion is "under-representation." For Asian applicants, they will have more slack as compared to Williams and Amherst. Thus, it is our opinion that an Asian applicant would have great chance of gaining admissions if his/her test scores are only at the 50 percentile. Furthermore, Asian student from CA would also have "geographic" advantage since Wesleyan likes to make itself more well-known in the West Coast. Thus, the combined ethnicity and geographic factors provides Asian students an extra boost in their application to Wesleyan.

Athletics

If we add sports as an additional factor, Asian student-athletes would be in high demand at Wesleyan (assuming good grades and test scores at least the 50 percentile in Chart C). 26% of Wesleyan students participate in its inter-collegiate teams. Furthermore, Wesleyan's athletics is usually the weakest among the "Little Three." Thus, it is reasonable to conclude that Wesleyan needs student-athletes to fill its team rosters.

How good of an athlete do you need to be to have an edge in admissions? Of course, the better athlete would be very appealing to the Admissions Committee. However, it is our belief that even an "average" athlete can enhance her/his chances to Wesleyan. That is because most of Wesleyan's athletic teams are "average" as compared to Williams and Amherst.

You Can Study Science as well as Liberal Arts

As shown on chart E above, plenty of Wesleyan students study math and science (17%). The smaller classes (9-to-1 student to faculty ratio) allows for better learning in math and sciences. Physical science majors (7%) is the most popular major among math/science majors. (Physical science is usually comprise of Chemistry or Physics). Another 5% study biology or related majors. Again, you can study science at a small school such as Amherst and still attend medical school or Ph.D. later.

Conclusion

In summary, the following "strategies" will increase your chances significantly at Wesleyan:

1) Asian students are "underrepresented" at Wesleyan (only 7%);
2) Thus, generally no need to apply for Early Decision, even if rate is higher than Regular Admission);
3) Instead, apply Early Decision (ED) to Williams or Amherst. If you are not offered acceptance through ED from Williams/Amherst, then apply to Wesleyan;
4) Student-athlete;
5) Apply to all majors. CA students have "geographic" advantage;
6) Ethnicity = Asian or International.

Bates College

A) Ethnicity

White	Asian	Race Unknown	Int'l Students
75%	5%	1%	6%

B) Admission Rates

Overall Admit Rate	Regular Admit Rate	Early Action/Early Decision
25%	NA	NA

C) Test Scores

SAT	**25 Percentile**	**75 Percentile**
Reading	620	710
Math	620	700
Writing	638	713
ACT	29	32

D) Financial Aid

% 1st Yr Student Receiving Grants	Avg Grants 1st Yr Student	Total Cost of Attendance (COA)
41%	$33,878	$55,300

E) Majors and Fields of Study

% Degrees in Math, Sci/Engr	Degrees in Other
17%	83%

Bates College

It is our assumption that most people (especially Asian students and parents) have never heard of Bates College. One reason we wrote this book is to introduce excellent and generous schools across the U.S. Thus, it is our hope that the definition of "good schools" is expanded after you finish reading this book.

Where is it?

Bates is located in Lewiston, Maine (2.5 hrs from Boston; 30 minutes from Portland, Maine). It is one of 3 Maine schools profiled in this book (the other 2 are Bowdoin and Colby). These 3 Maine school, along with Williams, Amherst and Wesleyan, are part of the NESCAC (New England Small Schools Athletic Conference). All members of the NESCAC (Middlebury is also a member) are liberal arts schools.

Money Matters

Let's talk about money. Bates offers a **61% discount** to qualified first-year students. And 41% of Bates freshmen students receive the discount ($33,878 vs. total COA of $55,300). If a fine school is offering a possible 61% discount, would you be at least interested?

Many parents and students mistakenly assume that liberal arts schools are "dead end" for careers. As we stated elsewhere in the book, that is absolutely not true. Bates graduates do very well? How well? Good enough to beat Columbia graduates in mid-career salary, according to www.payscale.com. That is NOT a misstatement. According to payscale.com, Bates graduates' mid-career salary (15 years after college graduation) is $99,800, just beating Columbia at $99,700. But Columbia's admission rate (HS Class of 2011) is 6.4%, while Bates is much easier to get into (Please see Chart B). Furthermore, Bates' $99,800 amount beats all other UC school except UC-Berkeley ($109K). We believe that Bates has "shown" us the money.

Ethnicity & Leverage

As shown on Chart A above, Bates is overwhelmingly white at 75% vs. 5% Asian. It is reasonable to conclude that Bates is looking to increase the Asian representation. Therefore, Asians (especially from the West Coast) would have an advantage – potentially big advantage – in admissions and financial aid.

Furthermore, Asians would have more "leverage" in financial aid as well. We all study leverage (physics) in high school. But leverage can be applied to everyday life. We refer to the title of this book (Education Judo). One "wins" if s/he can use leverage into his/her advantage.

Here, if an Asian student has test scores above the 50 percentile (please see Chart C), then we authors thinks that the chance of admissions would already be around 75%. From a leverage point of view, Bates would have to entice you the Applicant to attend. How? By offering more money (no different than the job market). Thus, it is highly likely that an Asian student (especially from CA) with 50 percentile numbers not only gains admissions, but also receives a financial aid offer with *more than* the amount in Chart D. For example, you could get 70% discount (similar to Williams and Amherst) off the sticker price. If you cannot get into Amherst or Williams, that would be a great offer from Bates.

Athletics

If we add sports as an additional factor, Asian student-athletes would be in high demand at Bates (assuming good grades and test scores at least the 50 percentile in Chart C). 45% of Bates students participate in its inter-collegiate teams. Many of these teams need student participation because each year, the senior graduates and some student with quit or study abroad. Thus, the largest available pool of participants would be freshmen students.

You Can Study Science as well as Liberal Arts

As shown on chart E above, plenty of Bates students study math and science (15%). The smaller classes (10-to-1 student to faculty ratio) allows for better learning in math and sciences. Biology and related major (8.5%) is the most popular major among math/science majors. Another 4% study Physics. Again, you can study science at a small school such as Bates and still attend medical school or Ph.D. later.

Conclusion

In summary, the following secrets will increase your chances significantly at Bates for admissions and financial aid:

1) Asian students are "underrepresented" at Bates (only 5%);
2) No need for Early Decision, because Asians has leverage;
3) Apply to all majors. CA students have "geographic" advantage;
4) Student-athlete.

Bowdoin College

A) Ethnicity

White	Asian	Race Unknown	Int'l Students
65%	7%	1%	4%

B) Admission Rates

Early Admit Rate	Regular Admit Rate	Early Action/Early Decision
15.8%	14.5%	28.9%

C) Test Scores

SAT	**25 Percentile**	**75 Percentile**
Reading	650	750
Math	660	750
Writing	660	750
ACT	30	33

D) Financial Aid

% 1st Yr Student Receiving Grants	Avg Grants 1st Yr Student	Total Cost of Attendance (COA)
47%	$37,640	$54,923

E) Majors and Fields of Study

% Degrees in Math, Sci/Engr	Degrees in Other
25%	75%

Bowdoin College

Among the 3 Maine schools profiled here, Bowdoin is the most competitive for admissions (see Chart B above). However, just as in the Ivy League, the "harder" to get in, the more financial aid a student can potentially receive. Furthermore, the ethnic mix of the students still favors Asian (please see Chart A).

Where is it?

Bowdoin is located in Brunswick, Maine (2.5 hrs from Boston; 30 minutes from Portland, Maine). It is also located half-hour from Bates College.

Money Matters & Career

For qualified students, Bowdoin is providing a 68.5% discount (more than Bates or Colby). Specifically, 47% of Bowdoin freshmen students receive the discount ($37,640 vs. total COA of $54,923). Thus, all 3 Maine schools offers at least 60% discount to qualified students. It is our opinion that these schools are indeed generous.

For career, Bowdoin graduates earns an average "mid-career" salary of $103K, beating all UC schools except UC-Berkeley ($109K). These figures are according to www.payscale.com. Furthermore, 6.5% Bowdoin students obtain PH.Ds subsequently, more than Dartmouth (5.7%) or UC-Berkeley (5.7%). These figures are according to the National Science Foundation.

Ethnicity & Leverage

The fact that Bowdoin has 7% Asian vs. 65% White (Chart A) great leverage for top Asian students. If your test scores are at 75 percentile (Chart C), you are like to gain admission with above average financial aid offer. Even if your scores are at the 50 percentile range, you still have a good chance of getting in. And if you do, an *average* grant offer of $37K would be even better.

Athletics

If we add sports as an additional factor, Asian student-athletes would be in high demand at Bowdoin (assuming you are a good student). Since 45% of Bowdoin students participate in its inter-collegiate teams, Bowdoin needs student-athletes to participate. Thus, you can leverage your athletic skills into an acceptance and nice financial aid package.

You Can Study Science as well as Liberal Arts

Many Bowdoin students study math and science. In fact, biology and related major (14%) is the most popular in all of Bowdoin, beating Economics (13%). Thus, students study "arts and science" in a liberal school like Bowdoin.

Conclusion

In summary, the following secrets will increase your chances significantly at Bowdoin for admissions and more financial aid:

1) Asian students are "underrepresented" at Bowdoin (only 7%). Male has slightly higher admission rate;
2) Apply to all majors. CA students have "geographic" advantage;
3) Although competitive, advise not to apply Early Decision because inflexibility;
4) Student-athlete.

Colby College

A) Ethnicity

White	Asian	Race Unknown	Int'l Students
60%	7%	19%	5%

B) Admission Rates

Overall Admit Rate	Regular Admit Rate	Early Action/Early Decision
30%	NA	NA

C) Test Scores

SAT	**25 Percentile**	**75 Percentile**
Reading	630	715
Math	630	715
Writing	620	715
ACT	28	31

D) Financial Aid

% 1st Yr Student Receiving Grants	Avg Grants 1st Yr Student	Total Cost of Attendance (COA)
40%	$34,449	$53,800

E) Majors and Fields of Study

% Degrees in Math, Sci/Engr	Degrees in Other
25%	75%

Colby College

Colby is probably another "unknown" school to many Asian students and parents. But it is fine school just like Bates College.

Where is it?

Colby is located in Waterville, Maine (3 hrs from Boston; 1.5 hr from Portland, Maine). It is also located 1 hour from Colby College. The other Maine college we are profiling is Bowdoin, located one hour away. Colby is a liberal arts school, just like Bates and Bowdoin.

Money Matters & Career

Offering a **64% discount** to qualified first-year students, Colby is generous. Specifically, 41% of Colby freshmen students receive the discount ($34,449 vs. total COA of $53,800).

For career, Colby graduates earns an average "mid-career" salary of $93K, beating UCLA ($91,600) and UC- Irvine ($92,500). These figures are according to www.payscale.com.

Ethnicity & Leverage

Since Colby only has 7% Asians vs. 60% White (please see Chart A), it is reasonable to conclude that Colby is looking to recruit top Asian students. Therefore, Asian students (especially from the West Coast) would have a significant advantage – potentially big advantage – in admissions and financial aid. As explained in the Bates section, this advantage can be leveraged into financial aid as well. Consequently, Asian students whose test scores at Colby's 50 percentile (please see Chart C) would have excellent chance of admission

Athletics

If we add sports as an additional factor, Asian student-athletes would be in high demand at Colby (assuming good grades and test scores at least the 50 percentile in Chart C). 41% of Colby students participate in its inter-collegiate teams. Many of these teams need student participation because each year, the senior graduates and some student with quit or study abroad. Thus, the largest available pool of participants would be freshmen students.

You Can Study Science as well as Liberal Arts

As shown on chart E above, plenty of Colby students study math and science (25%). The smaller classes (10-to-1 student to faculty ratio) allows for better learning in math and sciences. Biology and related major (14%) is the most popular major among math/science majors. Another 4% study Physics and math, respectively. Again, you can study science at a small school such as Colby and still attend medical school or Ph.D. later.

Conclusion

In summary, the following road map will increase your chances significantly at Colby for admissions and more financial aid:

1) Asian students are "underrepresented" at Colby (only 7%);
2) No need for Early Decision, because Asians has leverage;
3) Apply to all majors. CA students have "geographic" advantage;
4) Student-athlete.

Middlebury College

A) Ethnicity

White	Asian	Race Unknown	Int'l Students
67%	6%	5%	10%

B) Admission Rates

Overall Admit Rate	Regular Admit Rate	Early Action/Early Decision
18.5%	16%	42%

C) Test Scores

SAT	**25 Percentile**	**75 Percentile**
Reading	640	740
Math	650	740
Writing	660	750
ACT	30	33

D) Financial Aid

% 1st Yr Student Receiving Grants	Avg Grants 1st Yr Student	Total Cost of Attendance (COA)
41%	$32,934	$53,420

E) Majors and Fields of Study

% Degrees in Math, Sci/Engr	Degrees in Other
17%	83%

Middlebury College

Middlebury is part of NESCAC (New England Small School Athletic Conference), the same one that includes Williams, Amherst & Wesleyan. It is the only Vermont school (Middlebury, VT – 2.5 hrs from Albany, NY) we are profiling. With a total of 2,500 undergrads, it is also bigger than Amherst and Williams.

Money Matters & Career

In terms of financial aid, 41% of Middlebury freshmen students receive 62% discount off the sticker price. Against the total Cost of Attendance (COA) of $53,420, those qualified first-year students receive grants averaging $32,934, before any federal loans and work-study. Thus, the "out-the-door" price becomes approx. $20K ($53K-$33K), much lower than full-price for UC Schools.

For career, Middlebury graduates earn an average mid-career (15 years experience) salary of $93,600, more than highly ranked schools such Northwestern ($91,900) and Washington Univ.-St. Louis ($91,400). These figures are according to www.payscale.com. Thus, the quality of a Middlebury education is clearly on par with Northwestern and WUSTL. Furthermore, Middlebury graduates are expected to earn more than big schools such as NYU ($88,800) and Boston Univ. ($88,800).

Ethnicity & Leverage

As see clearly from Chart A, the demographics (6% Asians vs. 67% White) favors Asian applicants. Thus, we do not see a need to apply Early Decision unless Middlebury is you No. 1 school. Furthermore, since the demographics favors Asians, you merely need to be around the 50 percentile of test scores to get in (Chart C). You have even more leverage if you are an athlete.

Athletics

Just like other NESCAC and elite liberal arts schools, plenty of students (32%) participate in inter-collegiate sports. If you are an Asian student-athlete, it is our opinion that you can gain admissions even if your numbers are near the 25 percentile. This is based on the belief that White athlete applicants with similar numbers also have a good chance of getting in. Thus, Asian student-athletes have plenty of leverage.

You Can Study Science as well as Liberal Arts

Many Middlebury students study math and science. Biology and related major (9%) is the most popular math/science major at Middlebury, right behind Economics (11%). Thus, students study "arts and science" in a liberal school like Middlebury, and obtain PH.D's later.

Conclusion

In summary, the following road map will increase your chances significantly at Middlebury for admissions and more financial aid:

1) No need to apply Early Decision generally because Asians have leverage;
2) Apply to science and math majors;
3) CA students also have geographic leverage;
4) Student-athlete.

Haverford College

A) Ethnicity

White	Asian	Race Unknown	Int'l Students
69%	8%	0%	3%

B) Admission Rates

Overall Admit Rate	Regular Admit Rate	Early Action/Early Decision
25%	NA	NA

C) Test Scores

SAT	**25 Percentile**	**75 Percentile**
Reading	650	740
Math	650	740
Writing	660	750
ACT	30	33

D) Financial Aid

% 1st Yr Student Receiving Grants	Avg Grants 1st Yr Student	Total Cost of Attendance (COA)
52%	$34,673	$57,912

E) Majors and Fields of Study

% Degrees in Math, Sci/Engr	Degrees in Other
22%	78%

Haverford College

Now we are looking at 2 small liberal arts colleges outside Philadelphia, Haverford and Swarthmore (located 20 minutes apart). In this section, we will profile Haverford, which has a total enrollment of approx. 1,200 (all undergrads). As we stated in other parts of the book, a small school can pay "big" dividends.

Money Matters & Career

In terms of financial aid, those "dividends" include a **60%** discount off the sticker price to qualified students. Specifically, 52% of Haverford freshmen students receive the discount ($34,673 in grants vs. total COA of $57,912). And this amount is before any federal loans and work-study. After the "discount," the "out-the-door" price becomes approx. $23K ($57,912-$34,673), lower than full-price for UC Schools.

For career, Haverford graduates earns an average "mid-career" salary of $102K, beating all UC schools except UC-Berkeley ($109K). These figures are according to www.payscale.com. Furthermore, 9.7% Haverford students obtain PH.Ds subsequently, more than Williams (8.4%) or Duke (6.8%). These figures are according to the National Science Foundation.

Ethnicity & Leverage

The fact that Haverford has 8% Asian vs. 69% White (Chart A) great leverage for top Asian students. If your test scores are at 75 percentile (Chart C), you are like to gain admission with *above average* financial aid offer. Even if your scores are at the 50 percentile range, you still have a good chance of getting in. And if you do, the *average* grant for 1st year students is $35K.

Athletics

If we add sports as an additional factor, Asian student-athletes would be in high demand at Haverford (assuming you are a good student). Like other small liberal arts students, many students participate on sports teams. Since 47% of Haverford students participate in its inter-collegiate teams, Haverford needs student-athletes to participate. Thus, you can leverage your athletic skills into an acceptance and nice financial aid package.

You Can Study Science as well as Liberal Arts

Many Haverford students study math and science. In fact, biology and related major (10%) is the most popular in all of Haverford, the same as Political Science (10%). Thus, students study arts and science in a liberal school like Haverford, and obtain PH.D's later (see above).

Conclusion

In summary, the following strategies will increase your chances significantly at Haverford for admissions and more financial aid:

1) Asian students are "underrepresented" at Haverford (only 8%). Male has slightly edge (female =53%);
2) Apply to all majors. CA students have "geographic" advantage;
3) Although competitive, advise not to apply Early Decision because inflexibility;
4) Student-athlete.

Swarthmore College

A) Ethnicity

White	Asian	Race Unknown	Int'l Students
45%	14%	10%	7%

B) Admission Rates

Overall Admit Rate	Regular Admit Rate	Early Action/Early Decision
14%	NA	NA

C) Test Scores

SAT	**25 Percentile**	**75 Percentile**
Reading	670	760
Math	670	770
Writing	680	770
ACT	29	33

D) Financial Aid

% 1st Yr Student Receiving Grants	Avg Grants 1st Yr Student	Total Cost of Attendance (COA)
52%	$35,279	$55,530

E) Majors and Fields of Study

% Degrees in Math, Sci/Engr	Degrees in Other
23%	77%

Swarthmore College

Located 20 minutes part outside Philadelphia, Swarthmore is naturally a peer and rival of Haverford. Swarthmore has slightly higher enrollment at 1,500 (all undergrads). Both Haverford and Swarthmore "fight" with each other for ranking supremacy in *U.S. News and World Report* and similar publications.

Money Matters & Career

In terms of financial aid, 53% of Swarthmore freshmen students receive **63.5%** discount (slightly higher than Haverford's) off the sticker price. Against the total Cost of Attendance (COA) of $55,530, the average grant to those qualified first-year students is a sum of $35,279. Again, this amount is before any federal loans and work-study. After the "discount," the "out-the-door" price becomes approx. $20K ($57K-$35K), much lower than full-price for UC Schools.

For career, Swarthmore graduates earn an average "mid-career" (15 years experience) salary of $106K, the same as Cornell and Williams. These figures are according to www.payscale.com. Thus, the quality of a Swarthmore education is clearly on par with Cornell and Williams. Furthermore, according to the National Science Foundation. Swarthmore (12.9%) ranks No. 5 overall in likelihood of graduates obtaining PH.D's in science/engineering. That figures is higher than the well-known research school of University of Chicago (10.8%) and Stanford (8.1%).

Ethnicity & Leverage

However, Asians (with 14% vs. 45% White) would not have as much leverage as Haverford. Thus, an Asian applicant would need to be near the test scores at 75 percentile (Chart C). Clearly from Chart B, the admission rate shows that Swarthmore is more competitive than Haverford. Thus, it is suggested that applicants apply for Early Decision.

Athletics

Just like Haverford, Asian student-athletes would be in an advantageous position to Swarthmore if your scores are at least in the 50 percentile (Chart C). Furthermore, Swarthmore has men and women swimming teams while Haverford does not. Thus, that opens up another sport where Asian student-athlete can leverage upon.

You Can Study Science as well as Liberal Arts

Many Swarthmore students study math and science. Just like Haverford, biology and related major (12.5%) is the most popular at Swarthmore, beating Economics (12%). Thus, students study "arts and science" in a liberal school like Swarthmore, and obtain PH.D's later (see above).

Conclusion

In summary, the following "secrets" will increase your chances significantly at Swarthmore for admissions and more financial aid:

1) Male have slightly higher admit rate;
2) Apply Early Decision (especially female – only 14% admission rate);
3) Apply to science and math majors;
4) Student-athlete.

CONFERENCE THREE: Western Elite Schools

Our list of Western elite schools is headed by big-name schools Stanford, Cal Tech and USC, as well as 4 members of the Claremont schools. We are also profiling University of Pacific, Santa Clara University and Reed College.

From a financial point of view, they are quite generous. Please see the chart below:

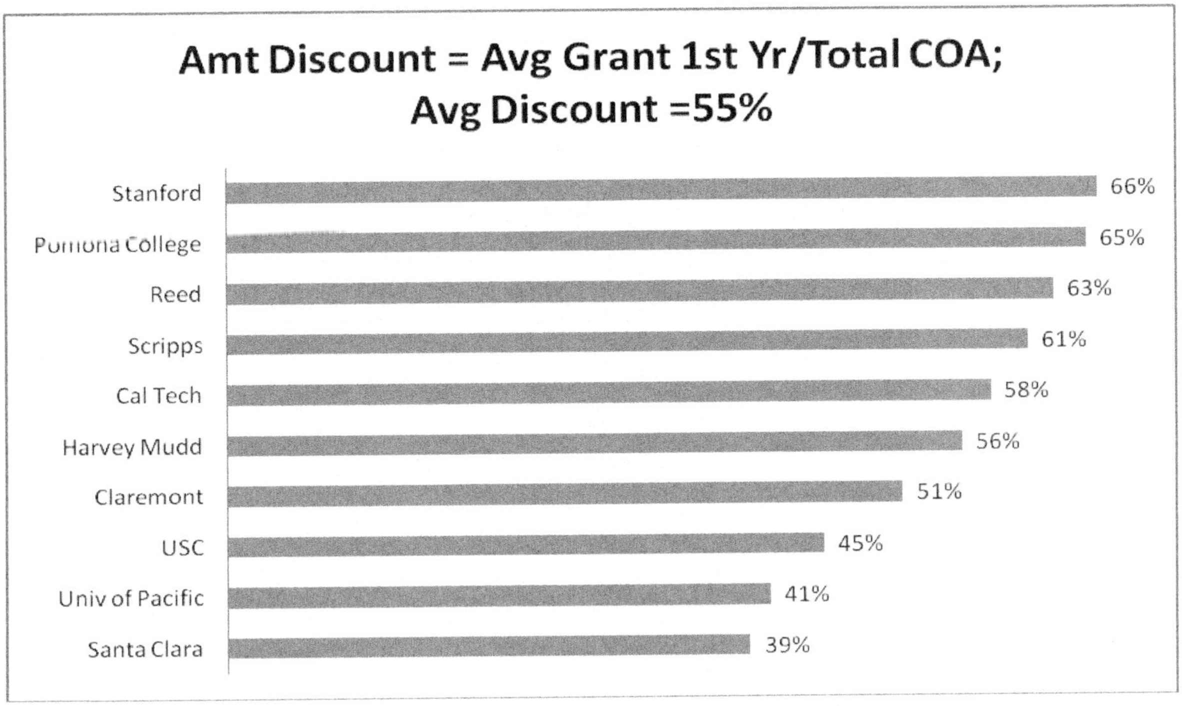

As expected, Stanford leads the way with a 66% discount to qualified students. In addition to a highly ranked school, Pomona (No. 6 in *U.S. News'* Liberal Arts rankings) is alos generous. Reed College, a school that many not be familiar, is actually more generous than Cal Tech and USC.

Thus, we are profiling famous and lesser-known schools. But they all are generous, one way or another. We are profiling this Conference in this order:

Western Elite Schools:

Stanford
USC
Cal Tech
Harvey Mudd
Pomona
Claremont McKenna
Scripps
Reed
Santa Clara
Univ. of Pacific

Stanford University

A) Ethnicity

White	Asian	Race Unknown	Int'l Students
34%	18%	8%	7%

B) Admission Rates

Overall Admit Rate	Regular Admit Rate	Early Action/Early Decision
6.63%	6.60%	13.0%

C) Test Scores

SAT	**25 Percentile**	**75 Percentile**
Reading	670	760
Math	690	790
Writing	680	780
ACT	31	34

D) Financial Aid

% 1st Yr Student Receiving Grants	Avg Grants 1st Yr Student	Total Cost of Attendance (COA)
53%	$37,804	$57,198

E) Majors and Fields of Study

% Degrees in Math, Sci/Engr	Degrees in Other
48%	52%

Stanford University

Among Asian parents and students, Stanford is probably the most desirable West Coast university. With its beautiful and large campus named the Farm, students can study for 4 years with other super-smart individuals and then create the next Yahoo, Google, etc. (if they have not done so already before they graduate). If graduates don't set up their own companies, the job opportunities in Silicon Valley are enormous.

Connection With Silicon Valley

Silicon Valley is perhaps the most fascinating job market in the work. In addition to being the "technology capital" of the world, it also has billions and billions of venture capital. Thus, you can think of Silicon Valley as a combination of Wall Street plus "society changing" technology. The next must-have product will likely come from Silicon Valley.

Stanford provides much of the intellectual talent for such innovations. Furthermore, with its strong alumni and connections, Stanford grads have little difficulty in finding employment. That is the primary reason that Stanford's popularity has risen so high, and admissions rates dropped to 7.1% this year (HS Class of 2011). In another words, 93 out of every 100 applicants get ***rejected***.

So for Asian students, what can be done to gain that "lucky" 7% acceptance? If you look at the Chart E: Majors and Fields of Study, you will see that almost half of Stanford (48%) studies math, science and engineering. Thus, there is almost an "even distribution" (50-50) of science and non-science majors.

Major as Leverage?

However, the authors researched the specific majors with the science and liberal arts category. And we have come to the following conclusions. First, biology and bio-related majors account for 21%, the largest major at Stanford. Thus, you must have stellar numbers and achievements to gain admission for a biology major. If not, you are likely to be the 93% that gets rejected.

Engineering students (all types) are only at 14% of undergrads at Stanford. So engineers would have a higher chance of getting in than bio majors. Third, liberal arts majors also provide better chance. For example, history (3.4%) and political science (4%) are majors that are below 5% at Stanford. Thus, if you are a history and *poli sci* (political science) major, you would have a better chance getting in Stanford, as compared to Harvard or Yale (much more history and political science applicants there).

Here is the list of certain majors with 5% or less Stanford students:

(a) Math – 3%;
(b) Physics – 5%;
(c) Computer Science – 5%;
(d) History – 3.4%;
(e) Political Science – 4%

Can sports help?

Not for the above-average athlete. Stanford's academic prowess is matched by all its athletic teams, who are higher ranked all across the board. Thus, among top schools in the U.S. (public and private), Stanford probably has the best combination academics and athletics teams. (For example, Stanford's football team was ranked in the top 10 last year, higher than any other school profiled in this book). Thus, athletics is not likely of help to any student (regardless of ethnicity), unless you are the very top of your sport (i.e. Olympic level).

Is Stanford generous?

Absolutely. Please see Chart D, where the average grant given to 1st students is almost $38K (53% of 1st year students receive this amount). That represents a 66% discount off the sticker price of Stanford.

Conclusion

In summary, the following strategies will increase your chances at Stanford:

1) Applying for Early Action (your chance would **double** that of the Regular Cycle);
2) Apply for math, physics, computer science, history or political science as major;
3) Do NOT apply as a biology or related major unless "extraordinary" credentials;
4) Race = unknown;
5) Do not present yourself as "well-rounded," Stanford is looking for exceptional students in a particular area. So put your best foot forward in one or two area;
6) Sports would NOT help most Applicants;

University of Southern California ("USC")

A) Ethnicity

White	Asian	Race Unknown	Int'l Students
44%	24%	2%	11%

B) Admission Rates

Overall Admit Rate	Regular Admit Rate	Early Action/Early Decision
18.2%	18.2%	No EA/ED Program

C) Test Scores

SAT	**25 Percentile**	**75 Percentile**
Reading	620	720
Math	650	750
Writing	640	740
ACT	29	33

D) Financial Aid

% 1st Yr Student Receiving Grants	Avg Grants 1st Yr Student	Total Cost of Attendance (COA)
63%	$26,112	$57,876

E) Majors and Fields of Study

% Degrees in Math, Sci/Engr	Degrees in Other
18%	82%

University of Southern California ("USC")

Here in Southern California, the no. 1 choice among Asian students and parents for local private schools is USC. Many parents have said that if their child can get into USC, cost is of little concern. Perhaps they should be concerned by the bill. The COA (Cost of Attendance) is now almost $58K (Please see Chart D above).

However, if you are able to get in (24% acceptance rate and decreasing; please see Chart A above), then there is a 63% chance you would receive an average of $26K in grants for the first year. Since many Asian parents are not even concerned about the costs, receiving $26K would "sweeten" any offer of acceptance to USC. Subtract $26K from the $58K total bill and the net amount $32K "out-of-pocket." This amount is comparable to the total COA amount from UC schools (see our specific UC sections later in the book)

From an ethnicity point of view, Asians are already "over represented." Please see Chart A above. Already at 24% as compared to 5% of the U.S. general population, Asians applicants must stand out and not be the average applicant. Therefore, an Asian applicant (especially from California) **must** be at or above the 75 percentile test scores in Chart C. If you are an Asian applicant from elsewhere (East Coast, Midwest, South), your numbers can be lower because USC is looking for "geographic diversity."

If you are an international Asian applicant (China, Korea, Taiwan, India, Japan, etc), your numbers also need to be close to the 75 percentile of test scores. This is because USC already has 11% international students. This percentage of international students cannot go up too much higher. Furthermore, Asian international students also compete against those coming from Europe and Latin American. Thus, USC is very competitive for international students as well.

Athletics

USC has one of the strongest athletic tradition of any school in America. Indeed, its teams are highly ranked and many USC athletes became professional athletes. Thus, an athlete would need to be "elite" to be of any help to your application.

Applying for Particular Major

Here is the list of certain majors with 5% or less USC students:
(a) Math – 1%;
(b) Physics – 0.5%;
(c) Computer Science – 1%;
(d) History – 1%;
(e) Political Science – 3%

Throughout this book, we have repeated emphasize the importance of applying the "right major" to increase your chances and USC is no different. Looking over the data from the National Center for Education Statistics, we see that most popular undergraduate major in USC is "business" at 26%. Furthermore, math, science and engineering only accounts for 18% (please see Chart E above). Thus, students (all ethnicities) who are strong in math, science and engineering should clearly apply for those majors.

More specifically, math majors only account for 1% of USC bachelor degrees. Same for Computer Science (1%). Physics is at **0.5%** (not a misprint). History is also low (1%) and same for Political Science (3%).

Again, if you have great interest in the above majors and have the grades and test scores to back that up, your chances of getting in to USC just increased significantly.

Conclusion

In summary, the following "secrets" will increase your chances at USC:

1) Apply for the above major where competition is lower;
2) Do NOT apply for business major unless your grades and test scores are much higher than 75 percentile numbers;
3) Sports would NOT help most Applicants;
4) Geographic diversity – Midwest, East Coast and South (all ethnicities);
5) "Spring Admission" – Indicate your willingness to take a semester off and delay your start at your dream school until spring.

A) Ethnicity

White	Asian	Race Unknown	Int'l Students
37%	39%	2%	12%

B) Admission Rates

Overall Admit Rate	Regular Admit Rate	Early Action/Early Decision
13%	NA	NA

C) Test Scores

SAT	**25 Percentile**	**75 Percentile**
Reading	700	780
Math	770	800
Writing	710	780
ACT	34	35

D) Financial Aid

% 1st Yr Student Receiving Grants	Avg Grants 1st Yr Student	Total Cost of Attendance (COA)
53%	$31,302	$54,090

E) Majors and Fields of Study

% Degrees in Math, Sci/Engr	Degrees in Other
98%	2%

California Institute of Technology, or Cal Tech as its famous nickname, is simply seeking (and attracting) highly intellectual math, science and engineering students. The professors at Cal Tech are literally top of his or her field. If you are admitted to Cal Tech, the school believes you have the potential to win a Nobel Prize. It is no wonder it has been consistently ranked in the top 10 in *U.S. News & World Report.*

As seen from the test scores, Cal Tech is looking for high achievers. Many Cal Tech graduates go on to obtain PH.D.'s, if they decide not to accept a nice job after graduation. While those numbers (admission rate and test scores) may be a bit intimidating, there are still ways to increase your chance at such a fine school.

First, there is a gender gap: 60% male and 40% female, which explains why females are more than twice as likely to gain admission than males (23% vs. 9%). 23% is almost 1 in 4 chance. That sounds much better than 9% (1 in 10 chance).

Ethnicity do not favor Asians, since they *outnumber* Whites in Cal Tech (39% Asians vs. 37% White; please see Chart A). Supposed you are an Asian male, what can you do to increase your chances? Again, we are assuming you are an outstanding student otherwise, scoring at least in the 75th percentile (Chart C).

Thus, picking a major becomes paramount. Please refer to Chart E, where it shows 98% of Cal Tech students study math, science or engineering. But 2% study something else. And what exactly are those 2% Cal Tech students study? According to the National Center for Education Statistics, those 2% amounts to 4 students out of 192 graduated (Academic Year 2009-10). Two of those students received degrees in "Business/Managerial Economics." Another two students studied economics. During the 2009-10 year, 191 students received bachelor degrees and those 4 were the exception to the math, science & engineering field. Consequently, if any student has a strong interest in economics, your chance at Cal Tech would be enhanced (even better if you are female).

Can Sports Help?

Unlike Stanford, Cal Tech's teams are not powerhouses in any sport. They are looking to be just "competitive." Furthermore, due to the small size of the student body, 33% of Cal Tech students play on its varsity teams. Put another way, they need athletes. Therefore, if you are an above average athlete (especially Asian male), you chance for admission just receive a boost (from the average 9% to possibly 30-40%). If you are a female Asian athlete, you are practically "in" even if your SAT/ACT scores are at the 25th percentile. Thus, the answer is: yes, sports DOES help (for both Asian males and females).

How About the $Money$?

The money from Cal Tech is generous. Its averages $31,302 against total COA (Cost of Attendance) of $54,090, or a 58% discount. 53% of first year Cal Tech student receives this amount. Given the bright employment prospects of a Cal Tech degree, or path toward PH.D., an investment in Cal Tech education in well worth it.

Conclusion

In summary, the following strategies will increase your chances at Cal Tech:

1) Applying for Early Decision;
2) Be female (23.2% admission rate vs. 9.2% for males);
3) Student-Athlete (no need to be at Stanford's level);
4) Apply for economics major;
5) Geographic diversity – from Midwest or South.

Harvey Mudd College

A) Ethnicity

White	Asian	Race Unknown	Int'l Students
58%	19%	5%	5%

B) Admission Rates

Overall Admit Rate	Regular Admit Rate	Early Action/Early Decision
17.1%	17.0%	20.0%

C) Test Scores

SAT	25 Percentile	75 Percentile
Reading	670	760
Math	740	800
Writing	668	760
ACT	32	35

D) Financial Aid

% 1st Yr Student Receiving Grants	Avg Grants 1st Yr Student	Total Cost of Attendance (COA)
49%	$32,248	$57,968

E) Majors and Fields of Study

% Degrees in Math, Sci/Engr	Degrees in Other
97%	3%

Harvey Mudd College

A school that specializes in math, science and engineering, Harvey Mudd is part of the five Claremont Colleges, renowned for their academic rigor. Harvey Mudd, however, it is not as well-known as it should. Many parents and students (all ethnicities) somehow believe that a university (big school) is a better place to study science and engineering.

2d Highest rate of PH.D.'s behind Cal Tech

According to the National Science Foundation's study in 2008, Harvey Mudd ranks 2d behind Cal Tech for percentage of graduates that would go on to obtain PH.D.'s. Specifically, 25% of Harvey Mudd's graduates obtain Ph.D.'s. In fact, Harvey Mudd is ranked decisively in front of MIT (3rd place with 16.6%). Based on this impressive statistic, it behooves parents and students to consider Harvey Mudd for math, science and engineering.

Show Me the Money?

49% of Harvey Mudd's first year students receive an average of $32,248 in grants, against a total COA of almost $58K. That still accounts for a 56% discount off the sticker price.

That is not all. According to www.payscale.com, Harvey Mudd graduates ranks **No. 1** among all school in the U.S. for mid-career salary (15 years after graduation) with $126,000. How do they do it? The authors believe the high rate of PH.D.'s (which leads to steady high-paying jobs) contribute mightily to this salary number. Yes, for mid-career salary, Harvey Mudd beat schools such as Princeton ($123K), Harvard ($121K), and Stanford ($119K). We believe that Harvey Mudd has shown you the money and is generous.

Student-Athlete

As part of the Claremont Colleges, Harvey Mudd students can take courses the other 4 colleges. Since each college's student body is quite small, then it makes that they have combined sports teams.

For the 5 Claremont Colleges, they are split into 2 teams: (1) Claremont McKenna – Harvey Mudd – Scripps; (2) Pomona – Pitzer. Thus, students from different college compete as one according to the respective pairing above. It should be noted that the C-M-S (Clarement/Mudd/Scripps) and P-P (Pomona & Pitzer) are classified as "Division III" athletics. That means generally those teams are not as strong as sports powerhouse like Stanford, USC or Duke. So the Claremont schools are looking for (and welcoming) athletes. Since admissions is so competitive, athletic skills will definitely help.

Conclusion

In summary, the following "secrets" will increase your chances at Pomona:
1) Be female (admission = 48%, almost half);
2) Apply for Early Decision (if male);
3) Geo-graphic diversity, from East Coast, Midwest or South;
4) Student-athlete (again, Olympian level is not necessary, so above average ability would enhance your application).

Pomona College

A) Ethnicity

White	Asian	Race Unknown	Int'l Students
46%	14%	15%	6%

B) Admission Rates

Overall Admit Rate	Regular Admit Rate	Early Action/Early Decision
12.82%	11.90%	25.3%

C) Test Scores

SAT	25 Percentile	75 Percentile
Reading	680	780
Math	700	780
Writing	n/a	n/a
ACT	29	33

D) Financial Aid

% 1st Yr Student Receiving Grants	Avg Grants 1st Yr Student	Total Cost of Attendance (COA)
50%	$36,005	$55,160

E) Majors and Fields of Study

% Degrees in Math, Sci/Engr	Degrees in Other
34%	66%

Pomona College

Pomona has been consistently ranked by *U.S. News & World Report* as one of the top (if not the top) liberal arts colleges in the West. Located in sunny Southern California, it is part of the 5 consortium of college, collectively known as the "Claremont Colleges."

Unfortunately, it is the authors' observation that many Asian parents do not consider Pomona as a "top school" because it is primarily a "liberal arts" school. Even when their kids are top students, many parents still has a certain belief that a liberal arts school carries less value than an "university."

So what exactly is a "liberal arts" school? Well, it may be surprising to the uninformed, but liberal arts schools also has math and science programs. Usually, in the U.S. these schools offers "arts and science", including math as part of their curriculum. Moreover, "liberal arts" schools are usually smaller in size, allowing students to get to know professors better. Thus, if Asian parents know of these facts, perhaps they would consider "liberal arts" school much more highly.

Majors

So back to Pomona, with its 7-to-1 student to faculty ratio, has been attracting record applications. What do they study? Actually 16% of Pomona students study biology or related majors. Thus, for bio majors, Pomona should be near the top of your list of schools. While there is no engineering degree, as seen from Chart E, 34% of Pomona students study math and/or science. Consequently, Pomona is a great school to attend to learn "science" as well as "arts."

How About the Money?

Many parents often do not consider private schools such as Pomona because they only look at the sticker price. However, the schools we are profiling in this book are all "generous." Thus, while private schools like Pomona's sticker price may be higher than UC school's, we should look at the "out-the-door" price.

According to Pomona, 50% of first year students receive an average of $36K against the total COA (Cost of Attendance) of $55K. That is a whopping 65% off the sticker price, which is **comparable or even exceed** some of the Ivy League schools (Please see our separate Ivy League section). Excluding any loans or federal work-study aid, your "out-the-door" price would be **only $19K** per year ($55K - $36K). We believe that this is a great number, as compared to public UC schools. The generosity of Pomona's financial aid is another reason why it is so highly ranked. The authors believe that Pomona should be one of the top schools that top students should consider.

Conclusion

In summary, the following "secrets" will increase your chances at Pomona:
1) Males have big edge (admission rate at 50% higher than Females);
2) Apply for Early Decision (especially for females);
3) Apply for math and/or science majors;
4) Student-athlete (26% participation by student body. Pomona is NOT looking for Olympians, so above average ability would enhance your application).

Claremont McKenna College

A) Ethnicity

White	Asian	Race Unknown	Int'l Students
48%	12%	20%	7%

B) Admission Rates

Overall Admit Rate	Regular Admit Rate	Early Action/Early Decision
12.42%	10.40%	29.0%

C) Test Scores

SAT	25 Percentile	75 Percentile
Reading	640	740
Math	670	740
Writing	n/a	n/a
ACT	29	33

D) Financial Aid

% 1st Yr Student Receiving Grants	Avg Grants 1st Yr Student	Total Cost of Attendance (COA)
42%	$35,419	$60,065

E) Majors and Fields of Study

% Degrees in Math, Sci/Engr	Degrees in Other
11%	89%

Claremont McKenna College

Claremont McKenna College ("CMC") is another school below the radar of Asian parents and students in California, even though it is *located* in Southern California. With a total enrollment of only 1,261, CMC has a low student to faculty ratio of 9-to-1, great for studying. So why the not-so-hot reception among Asian students and parents? Again, it is perceived as a "liberal arts" school only, and thus many parents and students think that career choices are limited. Again, we have refuted this assertion in various sections of this book.

Is it the Money?

CMC is generous. The average grants provided to qualified 1st year students (42%) is $35,419, against the total COA of $60K. Thus, CMS is slashing 60% off its sticker price to qualified students. Furthermore, according to payscale.com, the average mid-career salary for CMC is $104K, higher than all UC schools except UC-Berkeley. This $104K by CMC is also higher than Johns Hopkins ($90K) or Northwestern ($92K).

Athletics

Sports will clearly help an Applicant because CMC is part of the C-M-S sports teams (CMC, Harvey Mudd and Scripps). Thus, do not hesitate to show off your athletic skills. The willingness to participate in sports teams is important because in small schools, they need good athletes to compete. Furthermore, being part of a sports team foster bonding with your classmates.

Ethnicity

Asians only accounts for 12% at CMC. Curiously, 20% of CMS students are classified as "race unknown." The authors believe most of these 20% are likely to be Caucasian students, thus the actual percentage of White student is probably at 60% (as opposed to the reported 48%). If so, Asian applicants would have an advantage because Asians appear to be "underrepresented" at CMC.

Conclusion

In summary, the following "secrets" will increase your chances at CMC:

1) Apply for Early Decision (50% higher chance than Regular);
2) Ethnicity = Asian (please state that on application);
3) Since Asians are "under-represented," apply for major that interests you;
4) Student-athlete (again, Olympian level is not necessary, so above average ability would enhance your application).

Scripps College

A) Ethnicity

White	Asian	Race Unknown	Int'l Students
60%	9%	6%	4%

B) Admission Rates

Overall Admit Rate	Regular Admit Rate	Early Action/Early Decision
30.0%	30.0%	39.0%

C) Test Scores

SAT	**25 Percentile**	**75 Percentile**
Reading	640	740
Math	630	710
Writing	640	740
ACT	28	32

D) Financial Aid

% 1st Yr Student Receiving Grants	Avg Grants 1st Yr Student	Total Cost of Attendance (COA)
44%	$33,362	$54,900

E) Majors and Fields of Study

% Degrees in Math, Sci/Engr	Degrees in Other
26%	74%

Scripps College

Scripps College is a member of the famed Claremont Colleges. Perhaps due to the fact that it is a all-female school, it is not well-known among Asian students and parents. Indeed, Scripps only has a 9% Asian representation. This fact itself presents great opportunities for Asian students who are looking for a top-notch education and receive generous financial aid.

Financial Aid

Let's go straight to the money issue. Scripps awards an average of $33,362 to qualified recipients (44% of all 1st-Year students). Please see Chart D above. Against a total COA of $54,900, that is a **61% discount** of the total cost. We strongly believe that any top-notch school that provides at least a 50% discount of its sticker price is worth considering. Scripps beat this benchmark easily.

Ethnicity

As stated above, Asians would be considered "underrepresented" and hold an advantage in the application process. Based on the data in Chart A, it is safe to conclude that Scripps is looking to increase the number of Asian students. Furthermore, your test scores probably just need to be near the 50 percentile, and not the 75th percentile as shown on Chart C. Moreover, there is no need to apply early unless you are set on Scripps.

Athletics

Sports will clearly help an applicant because Scripps is part of the C-M-S sports teams (CMC, Harvey Mudd and Scripps). Thus, do not hesitate to show off your athletic skills. The willingness to participate in sports teams is important because in small schools, they need good athletes to compete. Furthermore, being part of a sports team foster bonding with your classmates.

Not Just "Arts"

As shown on chart E above, plenty of Scripps students study math and science (26%). Therefore, even if you are planning to attend medical school, you can study "bio-chemistry" – the hottest major these days – at Scripps and still attend medical school. Chances are you will obtain a higher GPA in Scripps than in UC schools, due to the fact Scripps has much smaller classes (9-to-1 student to faculty ratio).

Conclusion

In summary, the following "secrets" will increase your chances at Scripps and obtain even more financial aid:

1) No need to apply for Early Decision (Asians at 9% are "underrepresented" at Scripps);
2) Student-Athlete;
3) Asian students who are math and science majors (i.e. bio-chemistry) should apply because its less competitive than other schools and Scripps seeks top Asian students.

Reed College

A) Ethnicity

White	Asian	Race Unknown	Int'l Students
56%	6%	17%	5%

B) Admission Rates

Overall Admit Rate	Regular Admit Rate	Early Action/Early Decision
34.1%	NA	NA

C) Test Scores

SAT	**25 Percentile**	**75 Percentile**
Reading	670	750
Math	640	710
Writing	n/a	n/a
ACT	30	33

D) Financial Aid

% 1st Yr Student Receiving Grants	Avg Grants 1st Yr Student	Total Cost of Attendance (COA)
46%	$34,939	$55,700

E) Majors and Fields of Study

% Degrees in Math, Sci/Engr	Degrees in Other
23%	77%

Reed College

Located in Portland, Oregon, Reed College is an undiscovered "gem" school for most parents and students (regardless of ethnicity). However, once you get to know this small but excellent "liberals arts" and science school, you would want to place it near the top of your list. Furthermore, you must have heard of Steve Jobs, the founder of Apple. Steve Jobs attended Reed for one year before starting Apple.

Financial Aid

If you are looking for a "good deal," how does a **63% discount** sound? Please see Chart D. As you can see, Reed awards almost of $35K to qualified recipients (46% all 1st-Year students). Against a total COA of $55,700, that is a **63% discount** of the total cost. Put another way, the "out-the-door" price is $20,700 ($55,700 - $35,000), before student loans and/or federal work-study, which could decrease your payments even further.

Need further proof of "money" and academic success at Reed? According to the National Science Foundation (2008), Reed graduates ranks No 4. among all U.S. colleges/universities with the likelihood of gaining PH.D.'s (science). Specifically, 13.8% of Reed graduates went to obtain a science PH.D, just behind MIT (16.6%). Moreover, Reed's PH.D. rate (13.8%) is almost double that of Johns Hopkins (7.7%), a more "famous" university. As mentioned above, once you get to know Reed, it should be on your priority list of colleges.

Ethnicity

As stated above in Chart A, Asians would be considered "underrepresented" with only 6% and hold an advantage in the application process. Based on the data in Chart A, it is safe to conclude that Reed is looking to increase the number of Asian students. Therefore, unlike schools such as Brown or Columbia (where applying early = advantage), there is no need to apply early to Reed. If you are an Asian student with top scores (i.e. above scores in the 75th percentile – Chart C), you may even receive more money as an inducement to attend Reed. Even if your scores are near the 25th percentile numbers, you would still have a good chance of gaining admissions.

Not Just "Arts"

As shown on chart E above, plenty of Reed students study math and science (23%). The smaller classes (10-to-1 student to faculty ratio) allows for better learning in math and sciences. Bio-related majors (10.4%) is the most popular major among math/science majors

Conclusion

In summary, the following "strategies" will increase your chances at Reed and obtain even more financial aid:

1) No need to apply for Early Decision (Asians at 6% are "underrepresented" at Reed);
2) Reed has no inter-collegiate sports teams, so athletics would not matter;
3) Even if Reed is not on top of your list of schools, it should be a back-up for Asian students (only a short plane ride from Southern California and elsewhere);
4) If admitted and Reed provide your **more than the average** amount shown on Chart C, then Reed deserves serious consideration.

Santa Clara University

A) Ethnicity

White	Asian	Race Unknown	Int'l Students
42%	17%	18%	3%

B) Admission Rates

Male Admit Rate	Female Admit Rate	Early Action/Early Decision
60.4%	58.4%	NA

C) Test Scores

SAT	**25 Percentile**	**75 Percentile**
Reading	550	660
Math	570	680
Writing	n/a	n/a
ACT	26	30

D) Financial Aid

% 1st Yr Student Receiving Grants	Avg Grants 1st Yr Student	Total Cost of Attendance (COA)
35%	$22,031	$55,380

E) Majors and Fields of Study

% Degrees in Math, Sci/Engr	Degrees in Other
17%	83%

Santa Clara University

Located in the heart of Silicon Valley, Santa Clara University utilizes its great location to the fullest. While Santa Clara is probably not the top of most Asian students' application list, we believe it should be. Or least consider it as a "safety" school.

On the first look, Santa Clara's numbers are not that amazing. Its admissions rate is quite high (please see Chart A). Furthermore, its financial aid grants to first year students is below those of other school that we profiled. (Also, only 35% of first year student receive grants). So why we include Santa Clara on our list of "generous" schools?

The answer is leverage – the essential element is judo and in many aspects of life. Let's say your test scores are at the Santa Clara's 75th percentile numbers (Please see Chart C above). You are not likely to get into Stanford, a "maybe" at best for USC. And the same result for "top UC" such as UC-Berkeley and UCLA (i.e. not likely). Our observation is that most students go for "next tier" UC's such as UC-San Diego, UC-Davis or UC-Irvine.

However, we are saying that perhaps these students should consider Santa Clara. Why? Because you have an excellent chance of gaining admission, based on your high scores. Furthermore, Santa Clara wants to recruit you (the outstanding student) to boost their average SAT and ACT scores. Thus, they are likely to offer you money that is **much** more than the average listed on Chart D. This is leverage because you the student have "higher number" than the average at Santa Clara and thus you are desirable to them.

Let's say they offer you $30K to attend. Thus, the "out-of-pocket" expense would be $25K ($55K COA - $30K grant). That would be *less* than the typical UC cost of $30K. Thus, let us pose this question: between $25K "out-of-pocket" vs. $30K for UCI, what would you choose?

Mid-Career Survey

Perhaps this next number we provide will help with this decision. According to the website www.Payscale.com, the average Santa Clara graduate makes $104,000 per year in mid-career salary (15 years experience). That is **higher** than UC-Irvine ($92,500), UC-Davis ($90,700), or UC-San Diego ($99,700). It is even higher than UCLA ($91,600). As we analyzed, the fact that Santa Clara is located in Silicon Valley is great for employment opportunities. Thus, before students and parents dismiss Santa Clara, they should keep these figures in mind. Furthermore, Santa Clara is a much smaller school than the average UC school, thereby allowing you to get acquainted with professors and obtain good grades easier.

Conclusion

In summary, the following "secrets" will increase your chances at Santa Clara and receiving more than average grants:

1) Be Male (female = 53%);
2) Apply for math, science or engineering (total only 17%).
3) No need to apply Early Decision or Action, students at 75th percentile has "leverage" as discussed above

University of Pacific ("UOP")

A) Ethnicity

White	Asian	Race Unknown	Int'l Students
36%	31%	5%	3%

B) Admission Rates

Male Admit Rate	Female Admit Rate	Early Action/Early Decision
39.3%	37.2%	No EA/ED Program

C) Test Scores

SAT	**25 Percentile**	**75 Percentile**
Reading	510	630
Math	530	660
Writing	510	630
ACT	22	28

D) Financial Aid

% 1st Yr Student Receiving Grants	Avg Grants 1st Yr Student	Total Cost of Attendance (COA)
76%	$21,652	$52,830

E) Majors and Fields of Study

% Degrees in Math, Sci/Engr	Degrees in Other
27%	73%

University of Pacific ("UOP")

Located in Stockton, CA, University of Pacific ("UOP") has a total undergrad enrollment of about 3,700, with a male/female split of 45% vs. 55%. In recent years, UOP has gained popularity among Asian students (see Chart A), resulting in a 31% Asian student population. One academic feature especially attractive to Asian parents and students is UOP's accelerated pharmacy program. Ranked 99th by *U.S. News* in the latest college rankings, UOP offers a combined Bachelors/Pharmacy program in 5, 6 or 7 years.

Financial Aid

UOP really spreads financial aid around, by offering 76% of 1st-year students grants averaging $21,652. Against a total COA of $52,830, that is a **41% discount** of the total cost. Put another way, the "out-the-door" price is $31,178 ($52,830 - $21,652), before student loans and/or federal work-study. Coincidentally, that is the approximately cost of full-priced UC schools.

As for mid-career salary (15 years of experience), UOP scores very well with an average salary of $100K, a much higher-than-expect amount for a school that is "only" ranked 99th. Specifically, the $100K number has UOP tied with Univ. of Chicago (ranked 9th/$100K), Rice (ranked 17th/$100K), and beats Columbia (ranked 4th/$99.7K) and USC (ranked 23rd/$99.4K). This is an impressive achievement. The salary numbers are according to www.payscale.com.

As for Ph. D. rate, UOP is not ranked in the top-50 schools who graduates later obtain science/math Ph. D.'s. However, UOP still have a very nice salary figure as well as decent (41% discount) financial aid. Thus, we consider UOP a generous school.

Ethnicity

As stated above in Chart A, Whites only outnumber Asians by 5% (36% vs. 31%). Therefore, in order for acceptance, you would need to score in the 75th percentile in test scores (Chart C). Furthermore, males would have an advantage since UOP has 55% female. Furthermore, while Asian students may be "over represented," Asian student-athletes are not and would be considered an advantage.

Study Science and Liberal Arts.

As shown on chart E above, plenty of UOP students study math, science and engineering (27%). Among those majors, 16% UOP students major in Biology and relate majors, while 8% study Engineering. As for non-science/engineering major, Business (24%) and Health related (8%) lead the way.

Conclusion

In summary, the following "strategies" will increase your chances at UOP:

1) Be male (UOP has 55% females);
2) Student-Athlete;
3) Even if UOP is not on top of your list of schools, it should be a back-up for Asian students (solid mid-career salary numbers
4) Apply for math, science and engineering majors.

CONFERENCE FOUR: East Coast Elite (Small to Mid-Size)

In this section, we are profiling the other East Coast elite schools (Small to Mid-Size) that offer generous financial aid with top-notch academics. For financial aid, please see below:

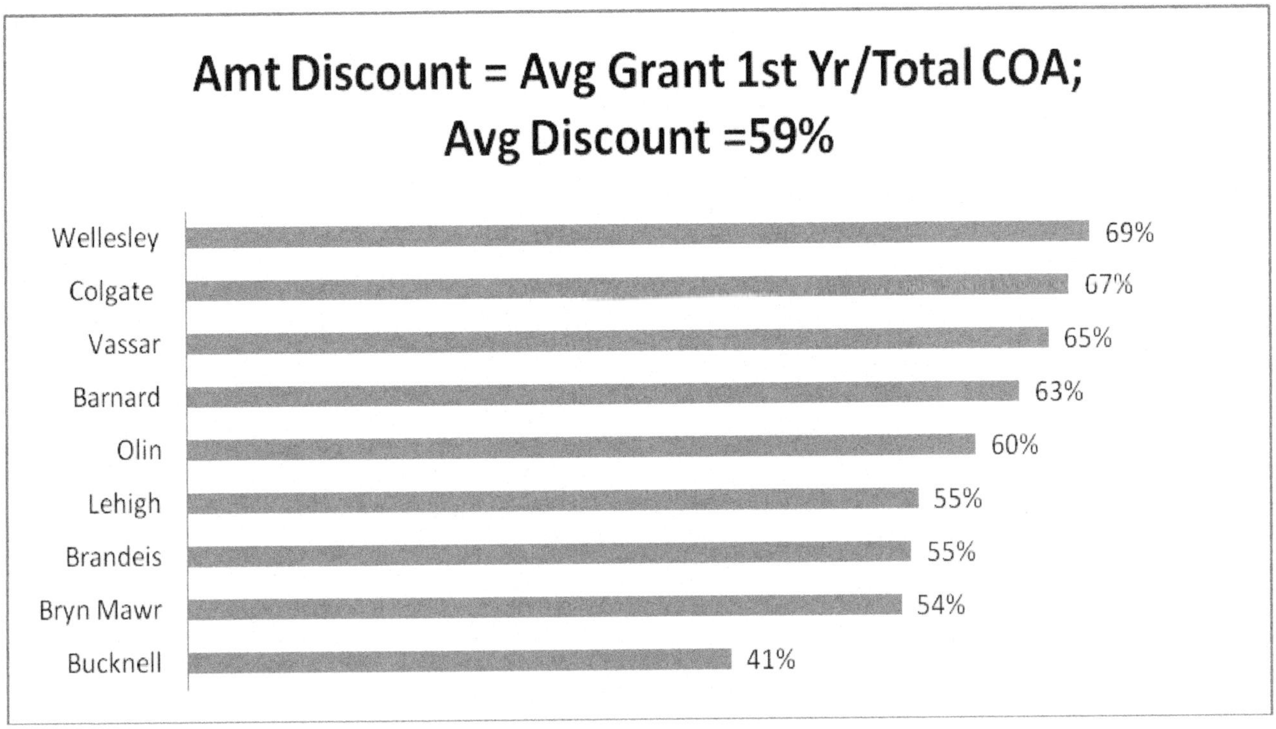

Among the above schools, Wellesley is probably the most well-known for Asian students and parents. And Wellesley does not disappoint with almost a *70% discount.* One reason we are writing this book is to introduce other fine schools to readers. You will see that other schools in the Chart will offer student a fine education as well as provide for generous financial aid.

We are profiling this Conference in this order:

East Coast Elite (Small to Mid-Size):

Wellesley
Barnard
Bryn Mawr
Vassar
Brandeis
Olin College of Engineering
Colgate
Bucknell
Lehigh

Wellesley College

A) Ethnicity

White	Asian	Race Unknown	Int'l Students
45%	21%	4%	11%

B) Admission Rates

Male	Female	Early Action/Early Decision
N/A	31%	58%

C) Test Scores

SAT	**25 Percentile**	**75 Percentile**
Reading	640	740
Math	730	740
Writing	650	750
ACT	28	31

D) Financial Aid

% 1st Yr Student Receiving Grants	Avg Grants 1st Yr Student	Total Cost of Attendance (COA)
61%	$36,508	$53,250

E) Majors and Fields of Study

% Degrees in Math, Sci/Engr	Degrees in Other
21%	79%

Wellesley College

Wellesley is perhaps the world's most famous all-female school. Boasting alumni such as former First Lady Hillary Clinton (and currently Secretary of State) and Madeleine Albright (former Sec. of State), Wellesley students are likely to be future leaders in government (either in U.S. or foreign). Wellesley should be well-known to Asians. Its 22% Asian populations supports this statement.

Financial Aid

Having a strong alumni network clearly helps financial aid, whose number are close to Ivy League's. Specifically, 61% of Wellesley 1st year students receive **69%** discount off the sticker price. Wellesley 69% discount is same as Princeton's to qualified students, and higher than Yale's (66%). Against the total Cost of Attendance (COA) of $53,250 those qualified first-year Wellesley students receive grants averaging **$36,508**, before any federal loans and work-study. Thus, the "out-the-door" price becomes approx. $16,742 ($53,250-$36,508), much lower than full-price for UC Schools.

Career & Alumni Network

Wellesley is internationally known, and thus attracting 11% international students. It should be noted that many of these international students are likely to be daughters of influential foreign politicians or businessmen. Thus, making friends with such classmates will widen your network no matter how your eventual career develops. Furthermore, many domestic students (White, Asian, Hispanic, Black) will likely to be leaders of this country in some capacity. Again, having friends in powerful places would only help.

6.5% of Wellesley graduates are likely to obtain science/math PH.D.'s (according to Nat'l Science Foundation). This figure is ahead of Dartmouth (5.7%) and UC-Berkeley (5.7%).

As for "mid-career" (15 yrs experience), one survey (www.payscale.com) reports $84,600. Although this number may seem "low," please keep in mind many Wellesley graduates work in the government, where the salary is lower. Furthermore, this number probably does not include wealthy and influential foreign graduates. As discussed above, Wellesley graduates wield plenty of political power. Thus, in this case, just putting a salary "number" on Wellesley graduates probably understate their success and influence.

Ethnicity & Leverage

Chart A clearly shows that Asian representation is only one-half of Whites. Thus, Asian do NOT have the usually leverage such as other East Coast schools (i.e. Bryn Mawr, Vassar, Bowdoin, etc.). So how does a female Asian applicant gain an edge into this influential and generous school? One factor (same as Ivy League) is sports.

Athletics

Just like the Ivy & NESCAC schools, participating in Wellesley sports teams shows that students are willing to "contribute" to the school. This is also important in development your network of contacts as your teammate will likely to be "famous." Therefore, think of it as another way to meet make friends and broaden your network.

A brief look at the Wellesley athletic website shows that Asian are well represented on sports teams. Thus, it is our belief that you need to be an above average athlete to gain an edge.

You Can Study Science as well as Liberal Arts

Many Wellesley students study math and science. Biology and related majors is most popular at Wellesley (14%), in front of Economics (13%). If you are wondering about biology, it is at 8%. Thus, students study "arts and science" in a liberal school like Wellesley, and obtain PH.D's later.

Conclusion

In summary, the following "road map" will increase Asian students' chances and financial aid significantly at Wellesley:

1) Apply Early (acceptance rate more than 50%);
2) If get in, great. If not, apply to other East Coast schools profiled here which Asians have "leverage);
3) CA students also have geographic leverage;
4) Student-athlete.

Barnard College

A) Ethnicity

White	Asian	Race Unknown	Int'l Students
65%	16%	0%	5%

B) Admission Rates

Overall Admit Rate	Regular Admit Rate	Early Action/Early Decision
20.97%	18.2%	44.8%

C) Test Scores

SAT	**25 Percentile**	**75 Percentile**
Reading	630	730
Math	620	720
Writing	650	750
ACT	28	32

D) Financial Aid

% 1st Yr Student Receiving Grants	Avg Grants 1st Yr Student	Total Cost of Attendance (COA)
42%	$36,670	$58,078

E) Majors and Fields of Study

% Degrees in Math, Sci/Engr	Degrees in Other
14%	86%

Barnard College

Barnard, an all-women college, is located right across the street from Columbia University (6.4% admission rate for 2011). According to Barnard's website, Columbia and Barnard shares an "unique" partnership.

Partnership with Columbia

Just like the Claremont Colleges, Barnard and Columbia students can take classes at each other schools. They shares libraries and work side-by-side in the same campus organizations. Furthermore, Barnard female athletes compete for Columbia's sports teams (Barnard has no stand-alone sports teams). Perhaps the most "unique" aspect of the partnership is that Barnard graduates receive diplomas *signed* by the presidents of both Columbia and Barnard.

Money Matters & Career

In terms of financial aid, 41% of Barnard freshmen students receive **62%** discount (as compared to **54% off** at Columbia) off the sticker price. Against the total Cost of Attendance (COA) of $53,420, those qualified first-year Barnard students receive grants averaging $32,934, before any federal loans and work-study. Thus, the "out-the-door" price becomes approx. $20K ($53K-$33K), much lower than full-price for UC Schools.

Ethnicity & Leverage

Since Columbia (6.4% admit rate) is almost as hard to gain acceptance as Harvard (6.2% admit rate), then getting into Barnard (27.8 admit rate – Chart A) is an easier "side door." The authors believe that of course one should try to gain acceptance to Columbia. But if that plan fails (almost 94% of time), then having Barnard as a "back-up" (if you are female) is not such a bad idea.

As for ethnicity, Asians (16% vs. 65% White) applying to Barnard would have slight edge, as opposed to applying to Columbia (15% Asians vs. 40% White). For Columbia, Asian students probably need test scores in the 99 percentile to get in (see Chart C). But for Barnard where Asian students have a slight leverage, we believe that 75 percentile test scores will be your "ticket" for Barnard acceptance.

Athletics

As noted, Barnard athletes compete for Columbia, which is not as strong as the Big Three is athletics overall. Those, Barnard (Columbia) would welcome Asian student-athletes who can "contribute." It is our opinion that Asian student-athletes would need to score in the 50 percentile test scores to gain admissions.

You Can Study Science as well as Liberal Arts

Many Barnard students study math and science. Biology and related major (9%) is the most popular math/science major at Barnard, behind Economics (13%). Thus, students study "arts and science" in a liberal school like Barnard, and obtain PH.D's later.

Conclusion

In summary, the following "road map" will increase your (female only) chances significantly at Barnard:

1) Apply to Early Decision to Columbia (if get in – great);
2) If not, then apply to Barnard;
3) CA students also have geographic leverage;
4) Apply to all majors;
5) Student-athlete
6) Ethnicity = Asian or International

Bryn Mawr College

A) Ethnicity

White	Asian	Race Unknown	Int'l Students
39%	12%	17%	12%

B) Admission Rates

Overall Admit Rate	Regular Admit Rate	Early Action/Early Decision
41%	N/A	N/A

C) Test Scores

SAT	**25 Percentile**	**75 Percentile**
Reading	590	720
Math	580	700
Writing	600	700
ACT	26	30

D) Financial Aid

% 1st Yr Student Receiving Grants	Avg Grants 1st Yr Student	Total Cost of Attendance (COA)
65%	$29,807	$55,200

E) Majors and Fields of Study

% Degrees in Math, Sci/Engr	Degrees in Other
24%	76%

Bryn Mawr College

Located just 10 miles outside Philadelphia is another fine school – Bryn Mawr. Again, this is another school that Asians students and parents in the West Coast know very little. If so, they would need to "catch up" because many international students know Bryn Mawr (12% of students). Bryn Mawr is all-female (same as Wellsley & Barnard) and is quite generous.

Money Matters & Career

Specifically 65% of Bryn Mawr 1st year students (higher than Yale's 58%, and just behind Harvard's 66%) receive an average grant of **$29,807**. Against the total Cost of Attendance (COA) of $55,200, that represents a 54% discount off the sticker price. Thus, the "out-the-door" price becomes approx. $25K ($55K-$30K), still **lower** than full-price for UC Schools. Again, the impressive number here is 64%: Bryn Mawr appears to spread financial to this numbers of students.

Bryn Mawr is ranked an impressive No. 11 for undergrads likely obtain a science/math PH.D. (according to the Nat'l Science Foundation). In fact, Bryn Mawr's rate (9.7%) ranks right behind Harvard (9.9%). Furthermore, Bryn Mawr ranks higher than more "famous" Stanford (8.1%) and Johns Hopkins (7.7%).

Ethnicity & Leverage

Chart A shows White/Asian ratio as 3.25 to 1 (39%/12%). However, it also shows 17% "race unknown." It is the authors' belief that the majority of such students are probably White, since Bryn Mawr is more well-known among Caucasians than Asians. Thus, Asian students still should have leverage, especially those from CA. Looking at Chart B & C, the admit rate is not impossible like Harvard/Yale/Princeton, etc. Specifically, the overall admit rate 48.7% is higher than UC-Berkeley (22%) and UCLA (25%). Thus, if a CA student cannot get in to those "top 2" UC Schools, then Bryn Mawr would serve as a nice back-up.

Furthermore, the test scores are reasonable. Throw in the leverage factor (from CA, sports, etc), Asian students would probably only need to score in the 50 percentile to secure an acceptance. Once, you would have a good chance to receive (64%) to receive its generous financial aid .

You Can Study Science as well as Liberal Arts

Many Bryn Mawr students study math and science. Biology and related major (8.5%) is the most popular math/science major at Bryn Mawr, behind English (11%). Thus, students study "arts and science" in a liberal school like Bryn Mawr, and obtain PH.D's later.

Conclusion

In summary, the following "road map" will increase Asian students' chances and financial aid significantly at Bryn Mawr:

1) No need to apply Early Decision because Asians have leverage;
2) CA students also have geographic leverage;
3) Apply to all majors;
4) Student-athlete
5) Finally, if CA resident, Bryn Mawr can serve as "back-up" to UC Schools.

Vassar College

A) Ethnicity

White	Asian	Race Unknown	Int'l Students
65%	9%	0%	6%

B) Admission Rates

Overall Admit Rate	Regular Admit Rate	Early Action/Early Decision
22.5%	20.7%	42.5%

C) Test Scores

SAT	**25 Percentile**	**75 Percentile**
Reading	670	740
Math	640	720
Writing	660	750
ACT	29	32

D) Financial Aid

% 1st Yr Student Receiving Grants	Avg Grants 1st Yr Student	Total Cost of Attendance (COA)
64%	$37,892	$57,925

E) Majors and Fields of Study

% Degrees in Math, Sci/Engr	Degrees in Other
20%	80%

Vassar College

Located just to the north of New York City (Poughkeepsie, NY), Vassar is ranked 12th by *U.S. News* for liberal arts schools. With approximately 2,500 students, there is a gender imbalance in favor of females (58%). Thus, as clearly shown on Chart B, males have a much admit rate than females (32.9% vs. 19.5%).

Money Matters & Career

In terms of financial aid, 64% of Vassar freshmen students receive **65%** discount off the sticker price. Against the total Cost of Attendance (COA) of $57,925, those qualified first-year Vassar students receive grants averaging $37,892, before any federal loans and work-study. Thus, the "out-the-door" price becomes approx. $20K ($57K-$37K), much lower than full-price for UC Schools.

Vassar is ranked in the top 50 (No. 43) in the likelihood of undergrads obtain a science/math PH.D. (from the Nat'l Science Foundation). In fact, Vassar's rate (5.6%) ranks right behind UC-Berkeley (5.7%).

Ethnicity & Leverage

Chart A clearly shows that Vassar is overwhelmingly White with 65% vs. 9% Asians. Thus, Asian will have leverage because Vassar is probably seeking to increase Asian representation. Consequently, it is our opinion that Asian applicant would only need 50 percentile test scores (Chart C) to have a great chance for admission. For male Asian applicants, that percentile should be even lower (since Vassar is only 42% Male). In fact, the higher male admit rate is reflected clearly in Chart B.

Athletics

It is our opinion that Asian student-athletes would be even in higher "demand" (especially male). As is the case with smaller schools, many sports teams need student participation and Vassar is no exception. For Asian student-athletes, your scores in the 50 percentile is almost a "sure ticket" in.

You Can Study Science as well as Liberal Arts

Many Vassar students study math and science. Biology and related major (8.6%) is the most popular math/science major at Vassar, behind English (10%). Thus, students study "arts and science" in a liberal school like Vassar, and obtain PH.D's later.

Conclusion

In summary, the following "road map" will increase Asian students' chances and financial aid significantly at Vassar:

1) Be male (but female will be favored as well due to 9% Asian only);
2) No need to apply Early Decision because Asians have leverage;
3) CA students also have geographic leverage;
4) Apply to all majors;
5) Student-athlete;
6) Ethnicity = Asian or International

Brandeis University

A) Ethnicity

White	Asian	Race Unknown	Int'l Students
48%	12%	17%	12%

B) Admission Rates

Overall Admit Rate	Regular Admit Rate	Early Action/Early Decision
35.4%	34.7%	48%

C) Test Scores

SAT	**25 Percentile**	**75 Percentile**
Reading	630	730
Math	640	730
Writing	640	730
ACT	28	32

D) Financial Aid

% 1st Yr Student Receiving Grants	Avg Grants 1st Yr Student	Total Cost of Attendance (COA)
58%	$30,543	$55,761

E) Majors and Fields of Study

% Degrees in Math, Sci/Engr	Degrees in Other
17%	83%

Conveniently located 20 miles from Boston, and 10 miles from Olin College, Brandeis is ranked 34th by *U. S. News*. If you are wondering why are we are profiling many schools from the Boston area, there is a good reason. Since the founding of Harvard in 1636, many other fine universities and colleges have been established near Boston. And Brandeis is part of that. Although it sometimes gets lost among the top schools such as Harvard and MIT, Brandeis is a "generous" school that offers excellent opportunities to students.

Financial Aid

Specifically 58% of Brandeis 1st year students receive an average grant of $30,543. Against the total Cost of Attendance (COA) of $55,761, that represents a 55% discount off the sticker price. Thus, the "out-the-door" price becomes approx. $25K ($55,761-$30,543), still **lower** than full-price for UC Schools.

Although considered a "liberal arts" school, Brandeis is ranked in the top 50 schools that is mostly likely to send its graduates to obtain science/math PH.D.'s Specifically, according to the National Science Foundation, 5.4% of Brandeis graduates (behind Dartmouth's 5.7%) do in fact obtain such PH.D.'s.

Ethnicity & Leverage

Chart A shows White/Asian ratio as 4 to 1 (48%/12%), with 17% race unknown. We believe that the majority of such students are probably White, since Brandeis is more well-known among Caucasians than Asians. Thus, Asian students still should have leverage, especially those from CA. Looking at Chart B & C, the approx. 36% admit rate is close to UC-San Diego's rate of 37% (please see UC-San Diego section).

However, it is the author's belief that a Asian applicant (from CA) would have a much BETTER chance to gaining admission into Brandeis than UC-San Diego, which has become much more competitive in recent years. As an Asian applicant to the UC schools, you don't really have much leverage. Again, you would have leverage if you apply to a school like Brandeis. Thus, it is the authors recommendation that Brandeis should serve at least as a back-up.

You Can Study Science as well as Liberal Arts

The more you get to know Brandeis, it just may become your first choice. Student Brandeis students study math and science. Biology and related majors (13%) is the most popular math/science major at Brandeis, same as Economics (13%). Thus, students study "arts and science" in a liberal school like Brandeis, and obtain PH.D's later. Further, Brandeis has a 9-to-1 student to faculty ratio. No UC Schools comes close. Lastly, only 9% of Brandeis classes have 30 or more students. As a comparison, the number for UC-San Diego is 45% (way too high).

Conclusion

In summary, the following "secrets" will increase your chances and financial aid significantly at Brandeis:

5) Asian male applicants should have "best" leverage (good chance of admission even w/ less than 50 percentile test scores);
6) No need for Asian applicant to apply Early Decision because of leverage;
7) CA students also have geographic leverage;
8) Student-athlete;
9) Apply for science and math majors.

Olin College of Engineering

A) Ethnicity

White	Asian	Race Unknown	Int'l Students
48%	12%	17%	12%

B) Admission Rates

Overall Admit Rate	Male Admit Rate	Female Admit Rate
17.7%	15%	70.3%

C) Test Scores

SAT	**25 Percentile**	**75 Percentile**
Reading	670	750
Math	710	780
Writing	650	730
ACT	33	35

D) Financial Aid

% 1st Yr Student Receiving Grants	Avg Grants 1st Yr Student	Total Cost of Attendance (COA)
65%	$35,310	$59,116

E) Majors and Fields of Study

% Degrees in Math, Sci/Engr	Degrees in Other
100%	0%

Olin College of Engineering

Olin is an "engineering-only" college, perhaps as a counter-balance to "liberal arts" schools. Located just 20 miles outside Boston, Olin is only 9 years old. Despite its young age, it has already attracted a high-quality student body. The 2 most unique features of Olin are (1) small student body – 350 total; and (2) half-tuition scholarship for all students.

Financial Aid

When Olin started in fall 2002, it gave "full tuition" scholarships to all students. That program was so successful (perhaps too successful) that Olin is now providing only "half-tuition" (currently worth **$19,500**) for all admitted students, regardless of financial need.

But that is not all, because as we know, tuition is only part of the COA (Cost of Attendance). With a total COA of $59,116, Olin provides more than the $19.5K in aid. In fact, it provides an average of **$35,310** (grants) to qualified students (65% of Olin students). That comes to a 60% discount off the sticker price.

Ethnicity & Leverage

Chart A clearly shows that females (45% of student body) has an excellent chance of gaining admission (70%) into Olin. With Asians (17%) being less than a 3-to-1 ratio to Whites (57%), Asians are still a bit underrepresented. Thus, Asian females has great chance of gaining admissions AND receiving a financial aid offer that is **above the average**. Reason: based on Chart A & B, Olin should be actively seeking Asian females.

Athletics

Currently, Olin has no inter-collegiate teams. However, Asian student-athletes still should gain an edge due to fact that sports serves as a balance to academics.

All Engineering with Small Classes

Olin is a school that offer degrees in engineering **only**. Thus, liberal arts majors would need to apply elsewhere. The fact that Olin has such a small student body allows student to receive personal attention from professors (9-to-1 student faculty ratio), much like a small liberal arts school. In fact, 42% of Olin classes has 9 or less students. Now that is the definition of "small classes." Although no research has been done, the authors believe that no other engineering school/department can claim such a figure

Conclusion

In summary, the following "road map" will increase Asian students' chances and financial aid significantly at Olin:

1) Asian females has perhaps 75% of admission (scores in 50 percentile, Chart C);
2) Asian males need to have test scores beyond 75 percentile;
3) CA students also have geographic leverage;
4) Ethnicity = Asian. International

Colgate University

A) Ethnicity

White	Asian	Race Unknown	Int'l Students
72%	4%	4%	6%

B) Admission Rates

Overall Admit Rate	Regular Admit Rate	Early Action/Early Decision
28.8%	26.6%	51%

C) Test Scores

SAT	**25 Percentile**	**75 Percentile**
Reading	630	720
Math	640	740
Writing	625	730
ACT	29	32

D) Financial Aid

% 1st Yr Student Receiving Grants	Avg Grants 1st Yr Student	Total Cost of Attendance (COA)
32%	$37,204	$55,570

E) Majors and Fields of Study

% Degrees in Math, Sci/Engr	Degrees in Other
15%	85%

Colgate University

Here is a guess, you as a reader probably never heard of Colgate University. Yes, it is located "in the middle of nowhere" in Hamilton, NY. It has an undergrad enrollment of approx. 2,900 with 59% female.

Where is that?

Colgate is located 1 hour from Syracuse (nearest big city). If Colgate's location is considered "isolated," then so is Cornell and UC-Davis. So we should not judge a book by its "cover."

Financial Aid

The primary reason why Colgate is profiled its generous financial aid and excellent academics. Specifically, qualified Colgate 1st year students (32%) receive an average grant of $37,204 (Chart D). Against the total Cost of Attendance (COA) of $55,570, that represents a nice **67% discount** off the sticker price. Thus, the "out-the-door" price becomes approx. $18K ($55K-$37K), **much lower** than full-price for UC Schools.

Although only 32% Colgate 1st year students receive this amount, it is the authors' opinion that that are many rich students attending such that they would subsidize other who need financial aid. This, this "32% issue" is actually beneficial for those who seek financial aid.

Want further proof of "showing you the money"? According to www.payscale.com, Colgate graduate mid-career (15 years experience) averages $119K. Yes, that figures beat all UC Schools, including UC-Berkeley ($109K). In fact, Colgate's $119K is ties with academic powerhouses Stanford and Duke. With that salary figure of $119K, Colgate *completely outdistances* themselves from higher ranked schools such as Washington University-St. Louis ($91K), Johns Hopkins ($90K), and Northwestern ($89K). At Colgate, they must been doing something right in "the middle of nowhere."

Ethnicity & Leverage

For admissions, Asians probably has **the most leverage** of any East Coast school we are profiling in this book. Please see Chart A, where 4% Asian are outnumbered even by 6% Internationals students (that shows Asians in this country knows less about Colgate than International students). With a 72% White student body, Whites outnumber Asians by 18-to-1. But that also means tremendous leverage for Asian students and applicants.

For Asian males, that leverage would be even greater since Colgate has 59% female. Thus, it is our belief that if Asian male applicant has close to 50 percentile test scores (Chart C), he is pretty "sure" to get in. Furthermore, he may even receive a financial aid package greater than the average amount of grant (Chart D). Thus, the "out-of-pocket" amount would be even less than the average $18K (see above).

Even for Asian female applicants, due to the fact there are so few Asian students (4%), you would still have great leverage. It is also out belief that 50% test scores would be enough (plus a decent essay of course) would get you in. Again, once "in," it is our belief that your financial aid package would be higher than the average in Chart D.

You Can Study Science as well as Liberal Arts

The more you get to know Colgate, it just may become your first choice. Student Colgate students study math and science. Biology and related majors (8%) is the most popular math/science major at Colgate, behind Political Science (9%). Thus, students study "arts and science" in a liberal school like Colgate, and obtain PH.D's later. Further, Colgate has a 10-to-1 student to faculty ratio. No UC Schools comes close. Lastly, only 9% of Colgate classes have 30 or more students. As a comparison, the number for UC-San Diego is 45% (way too high).

Conclusion

In summary, the following "secrets" will increase your chances and financial aid significantly at Colgate:

1) Asian male applicants should have "best" leverage (good chance of admission even w/ less than 50 percentile test scores);
2) No need for Asian applicant to apply Early Decision because of leverage;
3) CA students also have geographic leverage;
4) No need to be a Student-athlete (although it would help);
5) Apply for science and math majors.

Bucknell University

A) Ethnicity

White	Asian	Race Unknown	Int'l Students
81%	3%	3%	4%

B) Admission Rates

Male Admit Rate	Female Admit Rate	Early Action/Early Decision
30.2%	35.1%	N/A

C) Test Scores

SAT	**25 Percentile**	**75 Percentile**
Reading	590	670
Math	630	710
Writing	600	690
ACT	27	31

D) Financial Aid

% 1st Yr Student Receiving Grants	Avg Grants 1st Yr Student	Total Cost of Attendance (COA)
45%	$23,500	$57,140

E) Majors and Fields of Study

% Degrees in Math, Sci/Engr	Degrees in Other
35%	65%

Bucknell University

Ranked No. 30th by *U.S. News* for Liberal Arts colleges, Bucknell is located in Lewisburg, PA (3 hours from New York City and 2 hours from Lehigh University). Although classified as liberal arts by U.S. News, Bucknell has an engineering department. With an undergrad enrollment of just 3,500, Bucknell is 51% female and 49% male. We would venture to say that most of our readers have not heard of Bucknell.

Money Matters & Career

45% of Bucknell's 1st year students receive an average grant of $23,500. (Please see Chart D). Against the total Cost of Attendance (COA) of $57,140, that represents only a 41% discount off the sticker price. This is much lower than Lehigh's 55% discount.

As for mid-career (15 yrs experience), Bucknell graduates score exceptionally well, earning an impressive $115K. Bucknell's $115K is just below Stanford ($119K), but tops UPenn ($111K), Lehigh ($111K), Yale ($110K) and Brown ($109K). This is all according to www.payscale.com. Thus, Bucknell's graduates earn at or above Ivy Leaguers. Again, we are profiling schools that we consider to be hidden gems. When a school beats half the Ivy League in mid-career salary (and many other well-known schools), parents and students should take notice of Bucknell.

Thus, due to the excellent career prospects in terms of salary, Bucknell is a generous school.

Ethnicity & Leverage

Chart A clearly shows that Bucknell is overwhelmingly white with 81% vs. 3% Asians. Thus, Asian applicants will have great leverage because Bucknell is seeking to increase Asian representation. Consequently, it is our opinion that Asian applicant would only need 50 percentile test scores (Chart C) to have a great chance for admission. Since the ratio of Asians is so low, Asian applicant do not even need sports as leverage. Asian students in the 75 percentile of test scores should be to obtain financial aid package beyond the average (Chart D).

You Can Study Science as well as Liberal Arts

35% of Bucknell students study math, science and engineering (Chart E). Engineering (18%) and Biology (11%) make up most of those student at Bucknell. Among non-science/engineering majors, Economics (13%) is by far the most popular. Despite it's ranking in the "liberal arts" category, Bucknell's 35% in math, science and engineering is higher than all Ivy League schools except for Princeton (35%) and Cornell (42%).

Conclusion

In summary, the following strategies will increase your chances at Bucknell:

1) Ethnicity = Asian or International;
2) Apply to all majors;
3) CA students also have geographic leverage;
4) Females have slightly higher acceptance rate.

Lehigh University

A) Ethnicity

White	Asian	Race Unknown	Int'l Students
71%	6%	6%	5%

B) Admission Rates

Male Admit Rate	Female Admit Rate	Early Action/Early Decision
36.6%	39.6%	68.6%

C) Test Scores

SAT	**25 Percentile**	**75 Percentile**
Reading	580	670
Math	640	720
Writing	No data	No data
ACT	27	31

D) Financial Aid

% 1st Yr Student Receiving Grants	Avg Grants 1st Yr Student	Total Cost of Attendance (COA)
45%	$29,873	$54,020

E) Majors and Fields of Study

% Degrees in Math, Sci/Engr	Degrees in Other
43%	57%

Lehigh University

Time to discuss a school that has "University" in its name rather than a college. Lehigh Univ. (5,000 undergrads) is located in Bethlehem, PA (1.5 hrs from Philadelphia, and 1.5 hrs from Newark Int'l Airport). For those student who are looking to attend an engineering school, Lehigh has a formal engineering department.

Money Matters & Career

In terms of financial aid, 45% of Lehigh freshmen students receive 55% discount off the sticker price. Against the total Cost of Attendance (COA) of $54,020 those qualified first-year Lehigh students receive grants averaging $29,873, before any federal loans and work-study. Thus, the "out-the-door" price becomes approx. $24K ($54K-$30K), much lower than full-price for UC Schools.

As for "mid-career" (15 yrs experience), Lehigh graduates earn an impressive $111K, just ahead of Yale (110K). In fact, Lehigh's salary figures ranks much higher than "higher-ranked" schools such as Wash Univ-St.Louis ($91,400) and Northwestern ($91,900). Finally, Lehigh's $111K ranks higher than all UC Schools. This is all according to www.payscale.com. Thus, it is the author's opinion that sometimes the college "rankings" do not tell the whole story about a school.

Ethnicity & Leverage

Chart A clearly shows that Lehigh is overwhelmingly White with 71% vs. 6% Asians. Thus, Asian will have leverage because Lehigh is probably seeking to increase Asian representation. Consequently, it is our opinion that Asian applicants would only need 50 percentile test scores (Chart C) to have a great chance for admission. For Asian student-athletes, that percentile should be even lower (see below). Again, the Asian "leverage" relates to admission and obtaining a better than average financial aid offer.

Athletics

It is our opinion that Asian student-athletes would be even in higher demand, especially male. Therefore, for Asian student-athletes, you probably just need to score in the 25 percentile to obtain admissions.

You Can Study Science as well as Liberal Arts

Many Lehigh students study math and science. Engineering is the 2d most popular major (27%) behind business (30%) at Lehigh. If you are wondering about biology, it is at 8%. Thus, students study "arts and science" in a liberal school like Lehigh.

Conclusion

In summary, the following "road map" will increase Asian students' chances and financial aid significantly at Lehigh:

1) Be female (Lehigh = 59% male);
2) No need to apply Early Decision because Asians have leverage;
3) CA students also have geographic leverage;
4) Apply to all majors;
5) Student-athlete;
6) Ethnicity = Asian or International

CONFERENCE FIVE: East Coast Elite (Mid to Large)

In this section, we are profiling bigger schools that are likely to be more well-known to Asian students and parents. MIT, Johns Hopkins, NYU, Tufts are schools likely to be either dream schools or safety schools. Except for MIT, the financial aid discounts is not as high as smaller schools. Here is the Chart in detail:

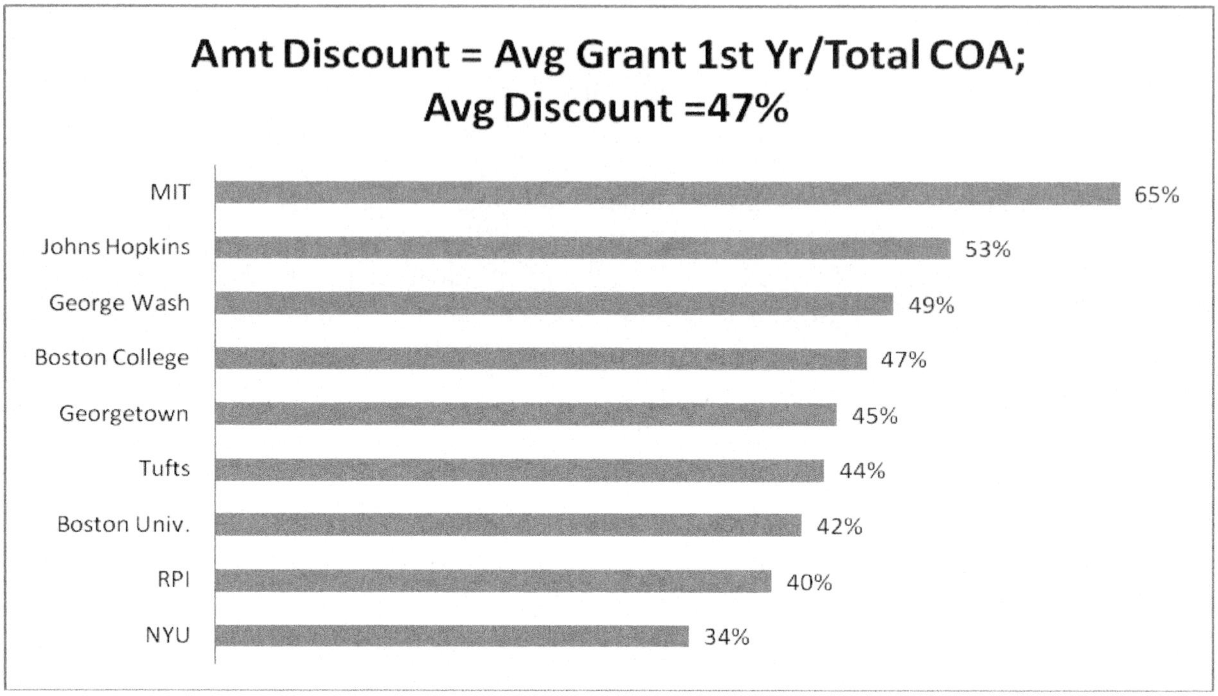

As a high ranking school, MIT (No. 7th by *U.S. News*) is also the most generous in this conference. Readers may be surprised to see that schools like NYU and Boston Univ. offering such low discounts. That is because they are already very well-known and they believe they do not need to offer discounts to entice students to attend. However, MIT is certainly well-known and it is offering 2/3 off the "sticker price." Reading this conference in detail will shatter many myths that readers may hold regarding these schools. We are profiling this Conference in this order:

East Coast Elite (Mid-Size to Large):

MIT
Boston College
Boston University
Tufts
Georgetown
George Washington
Johns Hopkins
NYU
RPI

Massachusetts Institute Of Technology ("MIT")

A) Ethnicity

White	Asian	Race Unknown	Int'l Students
37%	24%	5%	10%

B) Admission Rates

Overall Admit Rate	Regular Admit Rate	Early Action/Early Decision
8.95%	7.8%	11.3%

C) Test Scores

SAT	**25 Percentile**	**75 Percentile**
Reading	670	760
Math	740	800
Writing	670	760
ACT	32	35

D) Financial Aid

% 1st Yr Student Receiving Grants	Avg Grants 1st Yr Student	Total Cost of Attendance (COA)
65%	$36,084	$55,270

E) Majors and Fields of Study

% Degrees in Math, Sci/Engr	Degrees in Other
85%	15%

MIT

Massachusetts Institute of Technology (MIT) has one of the foremost academic reputations around the world. MIT and Harvard are the 2 most famous schools in the Boston area. Whereas Harvard focuses on liberal arts, MIT specializes in science and engineering. But this may be surprising to parents and students, MIT offers degrees in "liberal arts" as well. The gender gap of 10% at MIT (55% Male & 45% Female) is not as pronounced as compared to Cal Tech of 20% (60% Male & 40% Female). With an undergrad enrollment of approx. 4,200, MIT has an overall admit rate of only 9.6% (Chart B).

Financial Aid & Career Prospects

As a premier school, MIT is certainly generous. Specifically 65% of MIT 1st year students receive an average grant of $36K. (Please see Chart D). Against the total Cost of Attendance (COA) of $55K, that represents a 65% discount off the sticker price.

As for career prospects, MIT graduates receive a nice "payoff." Specifically, the average MIT mid-career salary (15 years experience) is $119K, right behind Cal Tech's $120K. (This is according to www.payscale.com). MIT's high salary figure is no doubt fuel by a high propensity of its graduates obtaining science/math/engineering PH.D.'s. According to the National Science Foundation, MIT is ranked 3rd among all U.S. Schools (Cal Tech 1st and Harvey Mudd 2nd) with 16.6% of its graduates obtaining such PH.D.s subsequently.

Ethnicity & Leverage?

Just like Cal Tech, ethnicity actually do not favor Asians, since they outnumber Whites in MIT (24% Asians vs. 37% White; please see Chart A). Clearly, Asian females has an advantage, due to MIT's gender gap. But suppose you are an Asian male, what can you do to increase your chances? Again, we are assuming you are an outstanding student otherwise, scoring at least in the 75th percentile in Chart C above.

Thus, picking a major becomes paramount. Please refer to Chart E, where it shows 15% of MIT student study subjects other than science, math or engineering. So what are those non-science and engineering majors? MIT's graduate business school has one of the best reputation in the U.S. So it is no surprising that business (7%) is the top major among non-science/math majors. Business and Economics (3%) account for 10% of MIT's undergraduate degrees. Therefore, the authors recommend applying for economics as major (if you have great interest in it), where you may gain a slight edge.

Applying for Early Decision also provides a slight advantage (12% admit rate vs. 8.2% Regular admit rate). Again, with top schools such as MIT, you need to apply Early Decision/Action to increase your chances. (Please also see our special section on Early Decision/Early Action).

Can Sports Help?

In a word: Yes. Just like Cal Tech, most of MIT teams are not powerhouses. They are looking to be just competitive. Furthermore, 17% of MIT student participate on its inter-collegiate teams. Thus, for Asian applicants, athletics would provide an edge (perhaps more of an edge than applying for a specific major as discussed above). For CA applicants, if you have played water sports (water polo, swimming), you should hold an edge because the standards for these two sports are higher than the East Coast. This is because water polo and swimming are year-round sports in CA; in the East, these sports are usually seasonal. (Please also see out special section on particular sports to focus on).

Consequently, we believe that even if you are "average athlete" by CA standards in water polo or swimming, your skills may be in high demand in a school such as MIT.

Conclusion

In summary, the following strategies/attributes will increase your chances at MIT:

1) Applying for Early Decision (12% admit rate vs. 8.6 Regular);
2) Be female;
3) Student-Athlete (indicate your willingness to participate, especially water sports);
4) Do something extraordinary, such as publication of scientific/engineering research;
5) Achievement in Math or Science (Intel or Siemens Contest, MITES, Math/Science Olympiad, AMC).

Boston College ("BC")

A) Ethnicity

White	Asian	Race Unknown	Int'l Students
65%	9%	9%	4%

B) Admission Rates

Overall Admit Rate	Regular Admit Rate	Early Action/Early Decision
28.9%	26.0%	N/A

C) Test Scores

SAT	**25 Percentile**	**75 Percentile**
Reading	610	700
Math	640	720
Writing	620	710
ACT	29	32

D) Financial Aid

% 1st Yr Student Receiving Grants	Avg Grants 1st Yr Student	Total Cost of Attendance (COA)
42%	$24,183	$56,922

E) Majors and Fields of Study

% Degrees in Math, Sci/Engr	Degrees in Other
12%	88%

Boston College ("BC")

Students in the West are sometimes confused between BC and Boston University ("BU"), thinking they are similar schools. Actually, they are very different. First, BC is about half BU's size, with total undergrad of approx. 10,000 (vs. 18,000 at BU). Ranked 31st by *U.S. News*, BC is more of a liberal arts school than BU. Second, BC is much more harder to get in (Chart B).

Financial Aid & Career Prospects

42% of BC's 1st year students receive an average grant of $26,556 (Chart D). Against the total Cost of Attendance (COA) of $56,368, that represents a 47% discount off the sticker price. (BU's discount=42%). BC's 47% discount is greater than fellow Catholic school Georgetown (45%), and another cross town rival Tufts (44%).

As for mid-career salary (15 years experience), BC graduates report an average of $96.8K, which about the same as Tufts ($96.4K) and UC-Santa Barbara ($96.4K). BC's salary number beats BU ($88.8K) and NYU ($88.8K) handily. As for Ph.D. rate, Boston College is not ranked in the top 50 schools whose graduates obtain science/engineering Ph.D. later. This is according to the National Science Foundation.

Overall, we like to see a school to provide a minimum 50% discount for qualified students. BC's 47% came close. BC's mid-career salary scored pretty well against area competitors. Thus, we conclude that BC is marginally generous. In financial aid & mid-career salary, BC bests BU in both of these categories. So BC is clearly better than BU in this regard.

Ethnicity & Leverage?

Chart A clearly shows Whites outnumber Asians by at least 7-to-1 (65% vs. 9%). Thus, Asians have more leverage (not as much as BU) when applying to BC. Furthermore, since many BC students are from the East, BC is certainly seeking to add more diversity to its student body. Specifically, looking at Chart A, Boston College should be seeking Asian and International students, as well as CA students.

BC's sports teams play in Division I (highest level), same as BU. Thus, you must be very good to make sports a factor. For Asians, ethnicity is a bigger "factor" than athletics.

You can Study Science/Engr and Liberal Arts

Chart E shows that 12% of BC students study math/science. 7.7% study biology. Among math/science majors, 21% study Business and another 9% study Communications. Please also see our section on Business as major.

Conclusion

In summary, the following "strategies" will increase your BC chances and financial aid offer;

1) Ethnicity = Asian or International;
2) Apply for math/science majors;
3) Student-Athlete probably would not help unless recruited;
4) CA students have geographic diversity advantage.

Boston University ("BU")

A) Ethnicity

White	Asian	Race Unknown	Int'l Students
47%	13%	19%	11%

B) Admission Rates

Overall Admit Rate	Regular Admit Rate	Early Action/Early Decision
45.5%	NA	NA

C) Test Scores

SAT	**25 Percentile**	**75 Percentile**
Reading	570	660
Math	600	690
Writing	590	680
ACT	26	30

D) Financial Aid

% 1st Yr Student Receiving Grants	Avg Grants 1st Yr Student	Total Cost of Attendance (COA)
46%	$23,413	$61,452

E) Majors and Fields of Study

% Degrees in Math, Sci/Engr	Degrees in Other
15%	85%

Boston University

For students looking for that "big city" college experience, Boston University is usually on top of their list (NYU is probably another school; please see its section separately). BU is also one of the largest private schools profiled here (approx. 18,000 undergrads). Furthermore, BU (60% female/40%male) has even a greater gender gap than George Washington. BU is well-known among Asian students and parents.

Financial Aid & Career Prospects

46% of Boston's 1st year students receive an average grant of $23,413. (Please see Chart D). Against the total Cost of Attendance (COA) of $61,452, that represents a 38% discount off the sticker price. (This is compared to 47% discount against cross-town rival Boston College). While 38% can be viewed as a bit low, BU is not an Ivy League school (avg. discount = 63%). Furthermore, BU is ranked 56th by *U.S. News & World Report*. Thus, 38% off can still be reasonable as "reasonable."

As for mid-career salary (15 years experience), BU graduates report an average of $88.8K, tied with NYU and close to UCLA ($91.6K). Given the fact that BU is ranked outside the top 50, its salary figure held up well against the other two "top 50" schools (NYU=33rd, and UCLA=25th). According to the National Science Foundation, BU is not ranked in the top 50 schools for rate of undergraduates obtaining science/math Ph.D.'s.

Ethnicity & Leverage?

With an approximately 60% admission rate (Chart B) and a low 9% of students, Asian have tremendous leverage when applying to BU. Furthermore, due to the **huge** gender gap, male Asian applicant have even greater leverage (admissions and financial aid). Consequently, an Asian male applicant having test scores in 50 percentile (Chart C) would likely gain admissions. If an Applicant wishes to receive an above average financial aid package (Chart D), s/he should have test scores in the 75 percentile.

BU's sports teams play in Division I (highest level). Thus, you must be very good to make sports a factor. For Asians, ethnicity is a bigger factor than athletics.

You can Study Science/Engr and Liberal Arts

Chart E shows that only 15% of BU students study math/ science/engineering, BU has its own engineering department (6% of students overall). 7% students study bio-related majors. Among non-science/engineering majors, 19% study Business. Please also see the section on "Business as Major."
As for class-size, only 16% of BU's classes have 30 or more students. This is *less* than the comparable number for MIT (23%).

Conclusion

In summary, the following "strategies" will increase your Boston chances;

1) Ethnicity = Asians (especially Male) but Asian female also has leverage;
2) Apply for math/science/engineering majors;
3) Student-Athlete probably would not help unless recruited;
4) CA students have geographic diversity advantage.

Tufts University

A) Ethnicity

White	Asian	Race Unknown	Int'l Students
47%	13%	19%	11%

B) Admission Rates

Overall Admit Rate	Regular Admit Rate	Early Action/Early Decision
21%	N/A	39%

C) Test Scores

SAT	**25 Percentile**	**75 Percentile**
Reading	670	740
Math	680	760
Writing	680	760
ACT	30	33

D) Financial Aid

% 1st Yr Student Receiving Grants	Avg Grants 1st Yr Student	Total Cost of Attendance (COA)
39%	$24,188	$54,866

E) Majors and Fields of Study

% Degrees in Math, Sci/Engr	Degrees in Other
21%	79%

Tufts University

Located just 8 miles outside Boston, Tufts is another fine school in the Boston area. With an undergrad enrollment of approx. 5,100, Tufts allows students to study liberal arts, science, math and engineering. It is ranked No. 28 by *U.S. News & World Report.*

Financial Aid & Career Prospects

39% of Tufts's 1st year students receive an average grant of $24,183. (Please see Chart D). Against the total Cost of Attendance (COA) of $56,922, that represents a 44% discount off the sticker price. This is comparable against cross-town rival Boston University (42%), but falls short against Brandeis (55%). While Tufts is not an Ivy league school (where the avg. discount = 63%), it is somewhat surprising that a school ranked so high (28th) is offering such a "low" discount.

As for mid-career salary (15 years experience), Tufts graduates report an average of $96.4K, right behind Boston College ($96.8K), and well ahead of Boston University ($88.8K) and Brandeis ($77.5K). Thus, this salary figure would at least hold up Tufts rankings. As for Ph.D. rate, Tufts is not ranked in the top 50 schools, whose graduates obtain Ph.D. in science/engineering later on, according to the National Science Foundation. As we discuss in other sections, we profiled many other smaller liberal arts school who are on such list so Tufts falters a bit in this category.

In summary, the financial discount is bit low, but Tufts graduates do have a fairly high mid-career salary. However, not enough students pursue Ph.D. from Tufts. Thus, we have to conclude that Tufts is not as generous as other schools we profiled here.

Ethnicity & Leverage?

Chart A shows Whites outnumber Asians by 5-to-1 (57% vs. 11%). With Tufts gaining in popularity, Asian applicants should have leverage, which would help since Tufts admissions rates are low (Chart B). That Chart also shows females have a higher admission rate. Consequently, an Asian female applicant having test scores in 50 percentile (Chart C) would likely gain admissions. If an Applicant wishes to receive an above average financial aid package (Chart D), s/he should have test scores in the 75 percentile.

Student-athletes with good grades and test scores will also have leverage. Tufts sports teams compete in Division III, and thus should welcome "above average" athletes. (Please see our special section on particular sports).

You can Study Science/Engr and Liberal Arts

Chart E shows that only 21% of Tufts students study science/engineering. The most popular one is Engineering (12%), followed by Biology (5%). Among non-science/engineering majors, 12% study International Relations and 8% study Economics.

Conclusion

In summary, the following strategies will increase your Tufts chances;

1) Asians have leverage, especially females;
2) Apply for math/science/engineering majors;
3) Student-Athlete has advantage;
4) CA students have geographic diversity advantage.

Georgetown University

A) Ethnicity

White	Asian	Race Unknown	Int'l Students
66%	9%	1%	7%

B) Admission Rates

Overall Admit Rate	Regular Admit Rate	Early Action/Early Decision
16.5%	15.04%	15%

C) Test Scores

SAT	**25 Percentile**	**75 Percentile**
Reading	650	750
Math	640	740
Writing	n/a	n/a
ACT	27	33

D) Financial Aid

% 1st Yr Student Receiving Grants	Avg Grants 1st Yr Student	Total Cost of Attendance (COA)
45%	$26,248	$58,300

E) Majors and Fields of Study

% Degrees in Math, Sci/Engr	Degrees in Other
9%	91%

Georgetown University

Located in within minutes of the White House in Washington, D.C., Georgetown's location and academics makes it a prominently ranked school (No. 21 according to *U.S. News &World Report*). Despite a relatively large undergrad size of approx. 7,000, it only has a low 10-to-1 student to faculty ratio. It also has a gender gap (55% female vs. 45% male). As a top-20 school, Georgetown should be well-known for Asian parents and students, even on the West Coast.

Financial Aid & Career Prospects

45% of Georgetown's 1st year students receive an average grant of $26,248. (Please see Chart D). Against the total Cost of Attendance (COA) of $58,300, that represents a 45% discount off the sticker price. Of course, other schools profiled in this book have much higher discounts. We are profiling Georgetown here because of its reputation.

As for mid-career salary (15 years experience), Georgetown graduates report an average of $104K. This figure is above all UC Schools except UC-Berkeley ($109K). This is according to www.payscale.com. Specifically, Georgetown's $104K figure is *above* cross-town rival George Washington (also profiled)'s $93K. Furthermore, Georgetown's $104K salary beats higher ranked Columbia ($99,700).

One main reason that students come to Georgetown is connections in government. And the best time to do it is in college. Thus, many of Georgetown's graduates work in the government, where salary are lower but whose influence are higher. Thus, this $104K should be adjusted upward.

Ethnicity & Leverage?

Chart A clearly shows Whites outnumber Asian by more than 7-to-1 (66% vs. 9%). Thus, Asians (especially from CA) have leverage. Furthermore, due to the fact females outnumber males by 10%, male Asian applicant have even greater leverage (admissions and financial aid). Consequently, an Asian male applicant having test scores in 75 percentile (Chart C) would likely gain admissions, AND receive an above average financial aid package (Chart D).

As for sports, Georgetown's sports teams are very good overall, especially its basketball teams (men & women's). Thus, unless you are a "top" player, sport would not be of much help.

Study Science/Engineering and Liberal Arts

Not surprisingly, International Relations is the most popular major (19%). But 9% students receive degrees in math/science at Georgetown. So even is international relation is not your "cup of tea," you can study math & science in a very small setting.

Conclusion

In summary, the following strategies will increase your Georgetown chances;

1) Ethnicity = Asians (especially Male) but Asian female also has leverage;
2) Apply for math/science majors;
3) Student-Athlete probably would not help unless recruited;
4) CA student have slight geographic diversity advantage.

George Washington University ("GW")

A) Ethnicity

White	Asian	Race Unknown	Int'l Students
55%	10%	12%	7%

B) Admission Rates

Overall Admit Rate	Regular Admit Rate	Early Action/Early Decision
32.6%	32.2%	38.2%

C) Test Scores

SAT	**25 Percentile**	**75 Percentile**
Reading	600	690
Math	610	700
Writing	620	700
ACT	27	31

D) Financial Aid

% 1st Yr Student Receiving Grants	Avg Grants 1st Yr Student	Total Cost of Attendance (COA)
45%	$28,704	$58,498

E) Majors and Fields of Study

% Degrees in Math, Sci/Engr	Degrees in Other
9%	91%

George Washington University

George Washington University is another big-city school. Widely known as "GW," it is located in the Foggy Bottom (U.S. State Department and White House) section of Washington, D.C. Despite its location, GW is not as well-known as it should, especially among CA Asian students and parents. GW is ranked 51st by *U.S. News*.

Financial Aid & Career Prospects

45% of George Washington's 1st year students receive an average grant of $28,704. (Please see Chart D). Against the total Cost of Attendance (COA) of $58,498, that represents a 49% discount off the sticker price. (This is compared to 45% discount against cross-town rival Georgetown).

As for mid-career salary (15 years experience), GW graduates report an average of $93.5K. This is according to www.payscale.com. Because of its location. many GW graduates work in the government, where the pay is lower but have jobs with stronger influence. Therefore, this $93.5K can be adjusted upward slightly. Furthermore, GW students have the tremendous opportunities for internships within the government or various national organizations located in Washington DC.

Even taking GW's $93,500 salary figure at face value, it is still ranked higher than schools such as UCLA ($91,600), UC-Irvine ($92,500) and Johns Hopkins ($90K). Thus, a GW degree more than hold its own in the market place.

Ethnicity & Leverage?

Chart A clearly shows Whites outnumber Asian by more than 5-to-1 (55% vs. 10%). Thus, Asians (especially from CA) have leverage. Furthermore, due to a **huge** gender gap (57% female/43%male), male Asian applicant have even greater leverage (admissions and financial aid). Consequently, an Asian male applicant having test scores in 50 percentile (Chart C) would likely gain admissions. If an Applicant wishes to receive an above average financial aid package (Chart D), s/he should have test scores in the 75 percentile (Chart C).

Like Georgetown, George Washington's sports teams play in Division I (highest level). Thus, you must be very good to make sports a factor. For Asians, ethnicity is a bigger "factor" than athletics.

Study Science/Engineering and Liberal Arts

While Chart E shows that only 9% of GW students study math/ science/engineering, GW has its own engineering department (3% of students overall). Thus, GW allows students to study engineering in small classes, which is not usually possible in many engineering schools (public or private). Another 4% students study bio-related majors. Among non-science/engineering majors, 20% study International Relations (big surprise).

Conclusion

In summary, the following strategies will increase your George Washington chances;

1) Ethnicity = Asians (especially Male) but Asian female also has leverage;
2) Apply for math/science/engineering majors;
3) Student-Athlete probably would not help unless recruited;
4) CA student have slight geographic diversity advantage;

Johns Hopkins University ("JHU")

A) Ethnicity

White	Asian	Race Unknown	Int'l Students
52%	21%	2%	8%

B) Admission Rates

Overall Admit Rate	Regular Admit Rate	Early Action/Early Decision
17.7%	16.2%	38.4%

C) Test Scores

SAT	**25 Percentile**	**75 Percentile**
Reading	630	740
Math	660	770
Writing	640	740
ACT	29	33

D) Financial Aid

% 1st Yr Student Receiving Grants	Avg Grants 1st Yr Student	Total Cost of Attendance (COA)
51%	$30,791	$57,942

E) Majors and Fields of Study

% Degrees in Math, Sci/Engr	Degrees in Other
61%	39%

Johns Hopkins University ("JHU")

Located in Baltimore, Maryland (1 hr. from Washington, DC), Johns Hopkins (JHU) has a premiere reputation for its science and engineering programs. Furthermore, JHU is also well-known among Asian students and parents.

Financial Aid & Career Prospects

First, 51% of Johns Hopkins 1st year students receive an average grant of $30,791. (Please see Chart D). Against the total Cost of Attendance (COA) of $57,942, that represents a healthy 53% discount off the sticker price.

As for mid-career salary (15 years experience), JHU graduates report an average of $90,100. This figure is somewhat surprising low for such a highly ranked school (No. 13 by *U.S. News & World Report*). The salary number is according to www.payscale.com. Specifically, JHU's $90K figure is *less* than UC-Davis' $90,700 and UC-Irvine's $92,500. According to *U.S. News & World Report's*, both UC-Davis (No. 39) and UC-Irvine (No. 41) are ranked well below JHU. Thus, this is a case where a school does not live up to its rankings.

As for likelihood of undergrads obtain PH.D. later, JHU actually score very well. 7.7% of Hopkins graduates are likely to earn PH.D. in science/engineering, according to the National Science Foundation. This figure is right behind Stanford (8.1%). But again, Stanford's mid-career salary of $119K beat JHU's $90K by a large margin (33%).

Ethnicity & Leverage?

With its reputation, JHU attracts many applicants, thereby resulting a admit rate of approx. 20% (Chart A). Furthermore, Asians (21%) are not under-represented at all. Chart B shows Early Decision admit rate is more than double Regular admission. Thus, if JHU is your 1st choice, apply Early Decision.

Can Sports Help?

Yes. As we discussed for completive schools, student-athletes often have an advantage and JHU is no different. But please keep in mind JHU is a national powerhouse is one sport – men's lacrosse (which is highly ranked year after year). For this sport, average athletes need not apply. Given the fact there are so few Asian in college sports, such student-athletes would be welcome and help your application. For example, CA applicants with experience in water sports (swimming, water polo) would be welcomed at a school like JHU.

Study Science/Engineering and Liberal Arts

Chart E shows that almost 40% of JHU students study majors other than science/engineering. Among those majors, Social Sciences (Political Science, International Relations, Economics) accounts for 16%. Psychology is at another 3%. Among science/engineering majors, Biology is at 13%. Bio-engineering has its own department and the rate is at 6.5%. So Biology and related majors accounts for almost 20% at JHU.

Conclusion

In summary, the following strategies will increase your JHU chances:

1) Applying for Early Decision (double chance of Regular Admission);
2) Be female;
3) Student-Athlete
4) CA student have slight geographic diversity advantage;
5) Apply for liberal art majors (political science, Asian studies) or physical sciences

New York University ("NYU")

A) Ethnicity

White	Asian	Race Unknown	Int'l Students
45%	20%	15%	7%

B) Admission Rates

Overall Admit Rate	Regular Admit Rate	Early Action/Early Decision
33.5%	26.7%	46%

C) Test Scores

SAT	**25 Percentile**	**75 Percentile**
Reading	610	710
Math	600	720
Writing	620	710
ACT	27	31

D) Financial Aid

% 1st Yr Student Receiving Grants	Avg Grants 1st Yr Student	Total Cost of Attendance (COA)
52%	$19,120	$55,542

E) Majors and Fields of Study

% Degrees in Math, Sci/Engr	Degrees in Other
6%	94%

New York University ("NYU")

For students looking for the ultimate "big city" experience, NYU would seem to have it all. Located right next to trendy (and expensive) Soho and Greenwich Village in Manhattan, students can study and party all night (even during weekdays). With an undergrad population of approx. 21,600, it is 61% female. Offering majors from business to the arts, NYU is ranked 31st by *U.S. News*.

Financial Aid & Career Prospects

52% of NYU's 1st year students receive an average grant of $19,120. (Please see Chart D). Against the total Cost of Attendance (COA) of $55,542, that represents a paltry 34% discount off the sticker price. This 34% "discount" is the lowest of any school profiled in this book. Indeed, no other schools is lower than 40%. Boston University, for example, offers 42% discount to qualified students. Many schools, especially those ranked above NYU, profiled here have discounts of above 50%. So this discount is somewhat disappointing.

As for mid-career salary (15 years experience), NYU also does not score so well. With a figure of $88.8K, NYU is tied with BU and close to UCLA ($91.6K). However, NYU is ranked about 20 places above BU in the *U.S. News* rankings. Furthermore, NYU's salary figure is beaten by UC-Berkeley ($106K), UC-San Diego ($99.7K), UC-Irvine ($92.5K), and UCLA ($91.6K). Even Cal Poly-San Luis Obispo's salary of dwarf $99.2K dwarf NYU's. These figures are according to www.payscale.com.

NYU is also not ranked in the top 50 of schools whose graduates are likely to obtain science/engr. Ph.D.'s, according to the National Science Foundation. Thus, based on the above factors, we conclude NYU is not a generous school.

Ethnicity & Leverage?

Chart A shows Whites outnumber Asian by about 2.5-to-1 (45% vs. 20%). Since many NYU students are from East Coast, Asians from CA would have leverage. Due to the fact that NYU has much more female students (61%), male applicants (regardless of ethnicity) have an advantage (See Chart A). Further, Asian student-athletes would have even greater leverage. Based on these factors, there is no need to apply for Early Decision.

You can Study Science/Engr and Liberal Arts

Chart E shows that only 6% of NYU students study math, science, and engineering. For those majors, biology is the top major (3%). For non-science/engineering majors, 22% study Performing Arts and 14% study Business. Please also see our special section on Business as major.

Conclusion

In summary, the following "strategies" will increase your NYU chances;

1) Be male;
2) Apply for math/science/engineering majors;
3) Ethnicity=Asian/International;
4) CA students have geographic diversity advantage.

Rensselaer Polytechnic Institute ("RPI")

A) Ethnicity

White	Asian	Race Unknown	Int'l Students
73%	11%	2%	4%

B) Admission Rates

Overall Admit Rate	Regular Admit Rate	Early Action/Early Decision
42.7%	43%	35.3%

C) Test Scores

SAT	**25 Percentile**	**75 Percentile**
Reading	610	700
Math	670	750
Writing	580	685
ACT	26	30

D) Financial Aid

% 1st Yr Student Receiving Grants	Avg Grants 1st Yr Student	Total Cost of Attendance (COA)
66%	$23,079	$57,179

E) Majors and Fields of Study

% Degrees in Math, Sci/Engr	Degrees in Other
80%	20%

Rensselaer Polytechnic Institute ("RPI")

Rensselaer Institute of Technology (RPI) is another East Coast school specializing science and engineering. Located 10 miles from Albany (NY) Int'l Airport, RPI is actually more conveniently located than many people realize. Ranked 41st by *U.S News*, RPI's is an excellent choice if you like to study science and engineering. With an enrollment of approx. 5,600, the male/female split is *72% vs. 28%.*

Financial Aid & Career Prospects

As for financial aid, 66% of RPI 1st year students receive an average grant of $23,079. (Please see Chart D). Against the total Cost of Attendance (COA) of $57,179, that represents only a 40% discount off the sticker price. As a comparison against other engineering schools, RPI's 40% "discount" is only close to Carnegie Mellon (43%). RPI falls way short against Case Western (46%), Johns Hopkins (53%), and MIT (65%).

As for mid-career salary, RPI's mid-career salary is reported as $109K, by www.payscale.com. This $109K beats all UC Schools. Furthermore, according to the National Science Foundation, RPI is ranked 34th among all U.S. Schools 6.4% of its graduates obtaining such PH.D. subsequently. This figure is below vs. in-state rival Cornell (7.6%) and against engineering peer Carnegie Mellon (7.1%). However, RPI's rate is above UC-Berkeley (5.7%) and Dartmouth (5.7%).

While the salary figure and Ph.D. rate is very good, the low average "discount" offer to students is a concern. Furthermore, the gender gap is way too *big* in favor of males (72%). Put another way, there are 2.5 male students for every female student at RPI. We are not aware of another co-ed school with such a big gender gap. With that in mind, the applicant (male or female) has to decide whether that RPI has the right social and academic environment. Thus overall, we can only conclude that RPI should be considered as a "back-up" school only.

Ethnicity & Leverage?

Chart A shows Whites outnumber Asians by about 7-to-1 (73% vs. 11%). Combined with the unbalanced gender ratio (see above), Asian female applicant have the most leverage. In fact, Asian female students probably just need to score in the 25th percentile in test scores (Chart C) to gain admissions. Asian males still have leverage because the relative low percentage of Asians overall. We don't believe Asian students need to rely on sports for RPI because of the great leverage they already have.

Areas of Study

54% of RPI students study Engineering, and another 9% study Computer Science. Among non-science/engineering majors, Business (7%) is the lead major.

Conclusion

In summary, the following strategies/attributes will increase your chances at RPI:

1) Asian female is almost sure to gain acceptance (25 percentile test scores = good enough);
2) Asian males (especially from CA) also have great leverage;
3) No need to apply Early Decision;
4) Correct approach would be to view RPI as back-up school.

CONFERENCE SIX: Mid-West Elite

Asian students are parents should be very familiar with highly ranked Midwest schools Northwestern, University of Chicago, and Washington University – St. Louis. They may not know about other premier schools in this conference. For financial aid, the Chart is as follows:

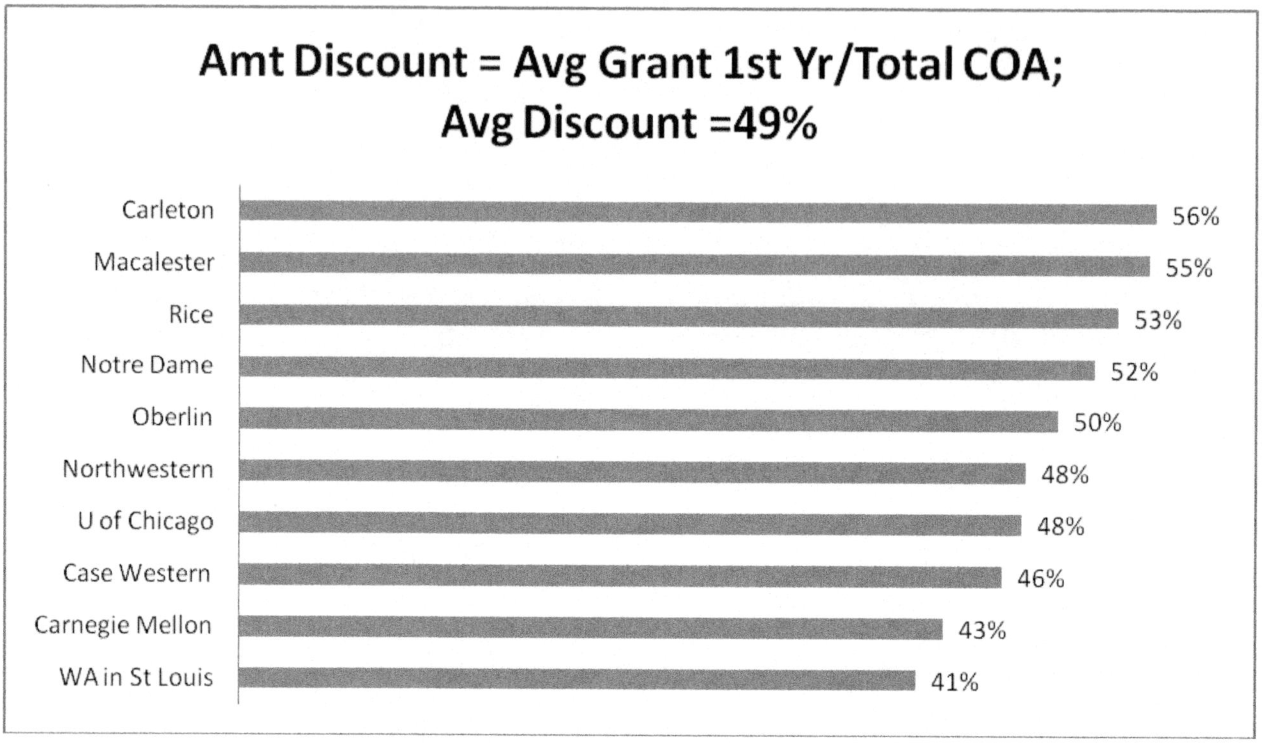

The school providing the highest discount is Carleton College, ranked No. 8 by *U.S. News* for Liberal Arts. If any reader knows Carleton and Macalester (55% discount above), s/he do *not* need to read this book. If you don't know Carleton and Macalester, then you really need to read on. There are also well-known schools such as Notre Dame, Carnegie Mellon and Rice, schools that may not be well-known but are undiscovered gems. We are profiling this Conference in this order:

Midwest Elite:

University of Chicago
Northwestern
Rice
Washington Univ. – St. Louis
Notre Dame
Oberlin
Carleton
Macalester
Carnegie Mellon
Case Western

University of Chicago

A) Ethnicity

White	Asian	Race Unknown	Int'l Students
43%	15%	18%	9%

B) Admission Rates

Overall Admit Rate	Regular Admit Rate	Early Action/Early Decision
13.2%	10.9%	18%

C) Test Scores

SAT	**25 Percentile**	**75 Percentile**
Reading	700	780
Math	700	780
Writing	690	770
ACT	30	34

D) Financial Aid

% 1st Yr Student Receiving Grants	Avg Grants 1st Yr Student	Total Cost of Attendance (COA)
60%	$28,068	$58,955

E) Majors and Fields of Study

% Degrees in Math, Sci/Engr	Degrees in Other
22%	78%

University of Chicago ("U of C")

University of Chicago (5,100 undergrads) is known for being an "intellectual school." This reputation is enhanced by the fact there are Nobel Prize winners in its faculty ranks. Ranked No. 9 by *U.S. News & World Report*, its reputation has been gaining, resulting in a more than 40% gain in applicants for 2011 HS Class.

Money Matters & Career

Offering a **48% discount** to qualified first-year students, U of C provides an average of $28K in grants (COA = $58,955, Chart D). U of C "spreads" this amount by providing it to 60% (vs. Northwestern's 48%) of 1st Year students.

For career salary, U of C graduates earns an average mid-career salary of $100K, beating peer schools such as Columbia ($99,700) and Northwestern ($91,900). These figures are according to www.payscale.com. Not surprisingly, U of C ranks No. 6 overall in the likelihood of its graduates obtaining science/engr. PH.D.'s (according to Nat'l Science Foundation). Specifically, 10.8% of U of C will earn science/engr. PH.D.'s. This number is ahead of Harvard (10.5%), Princeton (10.3%) and Stanford (8.2%). This is an impressive result. Thus, taking into account of financial aid and excellent career payoff, we believe U of C is generous and holds up its ranking very well.

Ethnicity & Leverage

So how can Asian students increase their chances for U of C? Chart A shows that Whites outnumber Asian almost by 3-to-1 (43% vs. 15%). However, there are also 18% race "unknown" students. We believe a majority of these "race unknown" are Asian and White. Thus, the real Asian percentage is probably understated. That means Asian ethnicity by itself is NOT enough for leverage.

Athletics

U of C's sports teams play in Division III (as compared to Northwestern in Div. I), and many of U of C's teams do *not* have strong traditions. Therefore, they would welcome decent to good athletes of any ethnicity. Thus, if you are an Asian athlete with 75 percentile in test scores, now you have a real chance of getting in. Whereas you are part of the "regular" pile, you may have moved yourself to the "athlete" pile. Furthermore, whereas athletics will not likely get you in at Northwestern (please see that section), athletics could be the deciding factor at U of C. Please also see our special section on particular sports.

You Can Study Science as well as Liberal Arts

As shown on chart E above, plenty of U of C students study math and science (22%). The small classes (*6-to-1* student to faculty ratio) allows for better learning in math and sciences. Bio-related majors account for 10% at U of C., and Economics (21%) is the most popular major overall. That is not surprising because several U of C faculty has won Nobel Prizes in Economics. Again, you can study science at a small school such as U of C and still attend medical school or Ph.D. later.

Conclusion

In summary, the following "strategies" will increase your chances at U of Chicago:

1) Apply for Early Decision (chance = higher);
2) Ethnicity = Asian or unknown;
3) Apply to all majors. CA students have "geographic" advantage;
4) Student-athlete.

Northwestern University ("NW")

A) Ethnicity

White	Asian	Race Unknown	Int'l Students
55%	19%	6%	6%

B) Admission Rates

Overall Admit Rate	Regular Admit Rate	Early Action/Early Decision
15.3%	13.8%	32.8%

C) Test Scores

SAT	**25 Percentile**	**75 Percentile**
Reading	670	750
Math	690	780
Writing	670	760
ACT	31	33

D) Financial Aid

% 1st Yr Student Receiving Grants	Avg Grants 1st Yr Student	Total Cost of Attendance (COA)
46%	$27,968	$58,429

E) Majors and Fields of Study

% Degrees in Math, Sci/Engr	Degrees in Other
24%	76%

Northwestern University

Northwestern ("NW"), along with Univ. of Chicago (ranked 9th), stands head and shoulders above other schools in the Chicago area. Located just outside Chicago in Evanston, Illinois, NW has an undergrad enrollment of approx. 8,600 (U of C = 5,100). Ranked No. 12th by *U.S. News & World Report* (behind University of Chicago), it is also well-known among Asian students and parents.

Money Matters & Career

For financial aid, 46% of NW's 1st year students receive an average grant of $27,968. Against a COA (Cost of Attendance) of $ 58,429, that is a 48% percent off the sticker price. As a comparison, 60% U of C 1st year students receive an avg. grant of $28,068.

For "mid-career" (15 years experience) salary, NW against falters vis-à-vis U of C. According to www.payscale.com, NW grads' salary of $91,900 falls about 10% short against U of C ($100K). Whereas U of C is ranked No. 6 in the likelihood of undergrads obtaining science/math PH.D.'s, NW is not ranked in the top 50.

The salary numbers at NW probably shows NW does not hold up its high ranking (13th) very well. Specifically, NW's $92K mid-career place it in the same "neighborhood" as Univ. of Scranton ($91,800; not profiled here), Loyola Marymount ($92,400; not profiled here), and St. Mary's of CA ($91,600; not profiled here). One would expect NW's mid-career salary to be much higher since it is ranked No. 12th. Thus, between University of Chicago and NW, U of Chi wins hands down.

Ethnicity & Leverage

Chart A shows Asian are at 19%, which is already above the percentage in other top schools (Ivy averages approx. 15%). Thus, Asians applying to NW don't have much leverage.

Above Average Athlete Need Not Apply

NW's team play in the Big Ten Conference (Div. I), one of the best athletic conferences in the entire U.S. Thus, you must be a "top, top" player in your sport to have any sort of leverage. If not, sports will not help you. If you are an "above average" athlete, you are better off applying to U of Chicago and probably can get in (test scores close to 75 percentile). That is why some students with "lower" scores may get into U of Chicago but not NW.

You Can Study Science as well as Liberal Arts

As shown on chart E above, plenty of Northwestern students study math/science/engr. (24%). In fact, 13% of NW students study engineering, and 3% study bio-related majors. Among non-science majors, Communications (17%) and Economics (12%) are the most popular.

Conclusion

In summary, the following strategies will increase your chances at NW:

1) Apply for Early Decision (chance = almost double Regular rate);
2) Be male (female = 52%);
3) Ethnicity = unknown;
4) Apply to science/math/engr.; CA students have "geographic" advantage
5) Student-athlete would not be much help.

Rice University

A) Ethnicity

White	Asian	Race Unknown	Int'l Students
44%	21%	6%	9%

B) Admission Rates

Overall Admit Rate	Regular Admit Rate	Early Action/Early Decision
16.0%	N/A	N/A

C) Test Scores

SAT	**25 Percentile**	**75 Percentile**
Reading	650	750
Math	690	790
Writing	660	760
ACT	30	34

D) Financial Aid

% 1st Yr Student Receiving Grants	Avg Grants 1st Yr Student	Total Cost of Attendance (COA)
68%	$25,581	$47,871

E) Majors and Fields of Study

% Degrees in Math, Sci/Engr	Degrees in Other
45%	55%

Rice University

With an undergrad total of approximately 3,300, Rice has the "feel" of a small college, although it is an "university." Conveniently located in the middle of the country (Houston, Texas), it is about a 3-hour flight from most of the U.S. Ranked No. 17th by *U.S. News & World Report*, Rice appears to be well-known among Asian students and parents (21% of study body).

Housing Modeled After Yale

Modeled after Yale's residential system, Rice students are randomly assigned to one of its ten residential colleges. The students would then share the same dining hall, same dormitory and same study hall – for their four years at Rice. Thus, a sense of community and bonding fostered through college.

Money Matters & Career

For financial aid, Rice spread the money around. Specifically, 68% (one of the highest % among schools in this book) of Rice 1st year students receive an average grant of $27,968. Against a COA (Cost of Attendance) of "only" $47,871 that come out to be a *53% discount* off the full price. Furthermore, Rice's COA is the **lowest** of any private school in this book. Even if you pay full price, Rice's COA is a "good deal."

For "mid-career" (15 years experience) salary, Rice grads average $100K, according to www.payscale.com. This $100K is same as U of Chicago, and above USC ($99,400), Univ. of Texas-Austin ($87,500), Washington U-St. Louis ($91,400).

Rice also ranks No. 9 (10.5%) among for likelihood of student obtaining science/engr. Ph.D., right on top of Princeton (10.3%) and Harvard (9.9%). Thus, all these and factors show Rice is "generous" and easily holds up its ranking.

Ethnicity & Leverage

Chart A shows Asian are at 21%, which is already above the percentage in other top schools (Ivy averages approx. 15%). Thus, Asians applying to Rice don't have much leverage. So Asian would need to rely on geographic diversity. According to Rice's website, 45% of its undergrads are from Texas. We believe that not as many Asian from CA are applying to this fine school (most Asians in Rice are from Texas or East Coast).

Above Average Athlete Need Not Apply

Rice sports plays in Div. I, so even for above average athletes, that would not be much help to anyone's application.

You Can Study Science as well as Liberal Arts

Chart E. shows that Rice is one of the most balanced school profiled here. With 45% students studying math/science/engr., you can study "arts and science." With a 6-to-1 student/faculty ratio, students will receive attention. Furthermore, 20% of Rice students study engineering, and 12.5% study bio-related majors. Among non-science majors, Economics (10.5%) lead the way.

Conclusion

In summary, the following "strategies" will increase your chances at Rice:

1) Apply for Early Decision (chance = 60% higher than Regular rate);
2) Be female (male = 52% at Rice);
3) Ethnicity = unknown;
4) Apply to all majors.; CA students have "geographic" advantage.

Washington University – St. Louis

A) Ethnicity

White	Asian	Race Unknown	Int'l Students
55%	19%	6%	6%

B) Admission Rates

Overall Admit Rate	Regular Admit Rate	Early Action/Early Decision
17.8%	16.5%	30.8%

C) Test Scores

SAT	**25 Percentile**	**75 Percentile**
Reading	680	750
Math	710	790
Writing	No data	No data
ACT	32	35

D) Financial Aid

% 1st Yr Student Receiving Grants	Avg Grants 1st Yr Student	Total Cost of Attendance (COA)
57%	$23,513	$56,930

E) Majors and Fields of Study

% Degrees in Math, Sci/Engr	Degrees in Other
28%	72%

Washington University – St. Louis

Washington Univ.-St. Louis ("WUSTL") is consistently ranked in the top 15 of *U.S. News & World Report* (latest ranking =13th). Well known among Asian students, WUSTL offers math/science/engineering program, and liberal arts. With an admit rate around 20% (Chart B), let's see if WUSTL is generous in terms of financial aid and career salary.

Money Matters & Career

For financial aid, 57% of WUSTL's 1st year students receive an average grant of $23,513. Against a COA (Cost of Attendance) of $ 56,930, that is **only 41%** (one of the *lowest* for top ranked schools) off the sticker price. As a comparison, Rice provides qualified students a 53% discount, mainly due to the fact that Rice's COA is approx. $9K lower (15% difference). We are somewhat mystified at the high COA for WUSTL. The cost of living in St. Louis should not be that much different from Houston. Cannot blame the maintenance of athletic teams for this; Rice's sports teams play in the competitive Div. I (i.e. football coach's salary > professor's). WUSTL's teams, meanwhile, play in Div. III (i.e. lower maintenance costs).

For mid-career (15 years experience) salary, the figure for WUSTL falls short of expectation of a top-ranked school. According to www.payscale.com**,** WUSTL grads' salary of $91,400 is barely ahead of UC-Davis ($90,700), which is ranked about 30 places lower. WUSTL also is no match against 17th ranked Rice ($100K) or 9th ranked Univ. of Chicago ($100K). Against acclaimed liberal arts schools, WUSTL does no better. For example, Pomona ($98K), Colby ($93K), and Amherst ($102K) all exceed WUSTL in this salary survey.

Then how about Ph.D. rate? Not that good either. WUSTL is not ranked in the top 50 schools for likelihood of undergrads obtaining science/engineering Ph.D. The schools ranked "around" WUSTL such as Johns Hopkins, Univ. of Chicago are all in the ranked in the top 50, according to the National Science Foundation. With the 50th ranked school (Hampshire College) at 5.3%, that means that this percentage for WUSTL is *less* than 5.3%.

Therefore, as compared to peer schools, WUSTL has a low discount for financial aid, and low salary prospects for such a highly ranked school. Thus, we believe that WUSTL is not that generous.

Ethnicity & Leverage

Chart A shows WUSTL Asian are at 19% (vs. 55% White), which is already above the percentage in other top schools (Ivy League averages approx. 15%). Thus, Asians applying to WUSTL don't have much leverage. So again Asian should increase leverage by…

Athletics

WUSTL's teams play in the Div. III (lest competitive), which is the same as MIT, Cal Tech and Univ. of Chicago (all Div. III). Since WUSTL is "hot" among Asian students, Asian applicant with 75th percentile test score may not get in. However, an "above-average" athlete with scores in the 75th percentile would greatly enhance his/her chance to WUSTL. As we discussed in other sections, Asian student-athletes are "under-represented at elite schools. Thus, sports would most likely help at WUSTL.

You Can Study Science as well as Liberal Arts

As shown on chart E above, plenty of WUSTL students study math/science/engr. (28%). In fact, 9.3% of WUSTL students study bio-related majors. Another12% study engineering. Among non-science majors, Business (12%) and Psychology (7%) are the most popular.

Conclusion

In summary, the following strategies will increase your chances at WUSTL:

1) Apply for Early Decision;
2) Be male (female = 52%);
3) Ethnicity = unknown;
4) Apply to science/math/engr.;
5) Student-athlete;
6) CA students have "geographic" advantage.

Notre Dame University

A) Ethnicity

White	Asian	Race Unknown	Int'l Students
74%	6%	1%	3%

B) Admission Rates

Overall Admit Rate	Regular Admit Rate	Early Action/Early Decision
22.7%	NA	NA

C) Test Scores

SAT	**25 Percentile**	**75 Percentile**
Reading	650	750
Math	680	760
Writing	640	730
ACT	31	34

D) Financial Aid

% 1st Yr Student Receiving Grants	Avg Grants 1st Yr Student	Total Cost of Attendance (COA)
51%	$28,799	$55,260

E) Majors and Fields of Study

% Degrees in Math, Sci/Engr	Degrees in Other
27%	73%

Notre Dame University

Most people probably heard of Notre Dame ("ND") because of its famous sports teams, especially football. But is also offers excellent academics. Ranked 19th by *U.S. News & World* Report college rankings, Notre Dame is located in South Bend, Indiana (2 hrs from Chicago). Sports is a such a dominant culture at Notre Dame. For CA students and parents, you can think of Notre Dame as USC of the Midwest. In fact, USC and Notre Dame have an annual football against each other.

Money Matters & Career

51% of Notre Dame 1st year students receive an average grant of $28,799 (Chart D). Against a COA (Cost of Attendance) of $55,260, that amounts to be a 52% discount off the full price. As a comparison, USC's discount is 45%. Notre Dame's 52% discount is also higher than Univ. of Chicago (48%), Northwestern (48%), Carnegie Mellon (43%), and Washington U-St. Louis (41%).

For "mid-career" (15 years experience) salary, Notre Dame grads average a "very high" amount of $112K, according to www.payscale.com. This $112K beats all other Midwest schools we are profiling in this book. It also beats all UC schools. Notre Dame's salary number has "no trouble" with USC's salary figure of $99,400. Against Ivy League schools, Notre Dame's salary beat Upenn ($111K), Yale ($110K), Cornell ($106K), Columbia ($99.7K), and Brown ($109K).

As for Ph.D. rate, Notre Dame is not ranked in the top 50 schools whose graduates are likely to obtain Ph.D.'s later on. This is according to Nat'l Science Foundation. However, given all of the above positive factors for Notre Dame, we conclude it is "generous" and easily holds up its ranking.

Ethnicity & Leverage

Chart A shows Whites outnumber Asians by 11-to-1 (76% vs. 7%). Thus, we can conclude Notre Dame would seek to recruit excellent Asian students, and thus Asians would have leverage. With that in mind, then Asian students would probably need to be around the 50 percentile test scores to gain acceptance (Chart C). If you like an above average financial aid offer, then you need to have test scores around 75 percentile.

Sports would be no help unless you are a "recruited" athlete (i.e. wanted badly by the coach). Notre Dame's athletic teams all have very strong traditions, with many team members becoming professional athletes (just like USC).

You Can Study Science as well as Liberal Arts

Chart E. shows that plenty of student study science/engineering at Notre Dame (27%). Specifically, for math/science/engineering, 9.3% study Engineering and 5.7% study Biology. Among non-science majors, Business (28%) is the overwhelming favorite.

Conclusion

In summary, the following "strategies" will increase your chances at ND:

1) Be female (male = 54% at Notre Dame);
2) Ethnicity = Asian/International
3) CA students have "geographic" advantage;
4) Apply to all majors;
5) Sports would not help, unless you are "recruited."

Oberlin College

A) Ethnicity

White	Asian	Race Unknown	Int'l Students
68%	6%	3%	5%

B) Admission Rates

Overall Admit Rate	Regular Admit Rate	Early Action/Early Decision
29.7%	NA	NA

C) Test Scores

SAT	**25 Percentile**	**75 Percentile**
Reading	650	750
Math	650	750
Writing	650	740
ACT	29	32

D) Financial Aid

% 1st Yr Student Receiving Grants	Avg Grants 1st Yr Student	Total Cost of Attendance (COA)
55%	$30,901	$57,025

E) Majors and Fields of Study

% Degrees in Math, Sci/Engr	Degrees in Other
35%	65%

Oberlin College

Located in its namesake town (Oberlin, Ohio), Oberlin College is only 40 miles from Cleveland, Ohio. With a total enrollment of. 2,900 (all undergrad), Oberlin is another fine but "lesser known" arts & science school. As with many smaller colleges, females outnumber males by 10% at Oberlin (55%-45%). Oberlin is ranked 23rd for liberal arts by *U.S. News*.

Money Matters & Career

55% of Oberlin freshmen students receive an average grant of $30,901. Against a total COA (Cost of Attendance) of $57,025, that amounts to a 54% discount. And this amount is before any federal loans and work-study. After the "discount," the "out-the-door" price becomes approx. $27K ($55K-$30K), still lower than full-price for UC Schools.

For career, according to www.payscale.com, Oberlin graduates earn an average "mid-career" salary of $80,800, a number certainly low as compared to other liberal arts schools. As for Ph.D. rate, Oberlin ranked 18th with a 8.4% rate, tied with Yale, and *ahead* of Stanford (8.2%). Furthermore, Oberlin's rate is also ahead of Cornell (7.6%) and Brown (7.4%). These figures are according to the Nat'l Science Foundation. While the salary number is low, the Ph.D. rates clearly show that Oberlin student are strong academically, similar to Ivy League schools.

Our interpretation is that a college degree by itself is not enough these days. A student needs to combine a bachelor degree with an advanced degree to "get ahead." Since approx. 20% study math/science at Oberlin (Chart E), and Oberlin has a 8.4% Ph.D. rate, that means out of those who study math/science, there is a higher chance for them to study Ph.D.

Ethnicity & Leverage

Asians has excellent leverage when applying to Oberlin. As seen on Chart A, Whites outnumber Asian 18-to-1 (72% vs. 4%). If your test scores are at 75 percentile (Chart C), you are like to gain admission with *above average* financial aid offer. Even if your scores are at the 50 percentile range, you still have a good chance of getting in (especially Male Asian).

Athletics

If we add sports as an additional factor, Asian student-athletes would be in high demand at Oberlin (assuming you are a good student). However, we believe Asian ethnicity is "big" enough of a factor already.

You Can Study Science as well as Liberal Arts

Many Oberlin students study math and science (20% - See Chart E). In fact, biology and related major (12%) is the most popular in all of Oberlin, the same as Music (12.5%). Thus, students study "arts and science" in a liberal school like Oberlin, and obtain PH.D's later (see above).

Conclusion

In summary, the following "secrets" will increase your chances significantly at Oberlin for admissions and more financial aid:

1) Asian students are "underrepresented" at Oberlin (only 4%);
2) Be male;
3) Apply to all majors. CA students have "geographic" advantage;
4) No need to apply Early Decision because Asians have leverage;
5) Student-athlete.

Carleton College

A) Ethnicity

White	Asian	Race Unknown	Int'l Students
68%	6%	3%	8%

B) Admission Rates

Overall Admit Rate	Regular Admit Rate	Early Action/Early Decision
25.6%	25.50%	40.50%

C) Test Scores

SAT	**25 Percentile**	**75 Percentile**
Reading	660	750
Math	660	760
Writing	660	750
ACT	29	33

D) Financial Aid

% 1st Yr Student Receiving Grants	Avg Grants 1st Yr Student	Total Cost of Attendance (COA)
52%	$30,179	$54,180

E) Majors and Fields of Study

% Degrees in Math, Sci/Engr	Degrees in Other
32%	68%

Carleton College

Located in Northfield, Minnesota, Carleton is another fine but "below the radar" school, especially to many Asian students and parents. Ranked 8th by *U.S. News* for liberal arts, Carleton is located only 40 miles from Minneapolis, MN (a big regional hub for airlines). With an enrollment of 2,000 (all undergrad), it is actually close in gender gap (52% female/48% male).

Money Matters & Career

52% of Carleton freshmen students receive an average grant of $30,179. Against a total COA (Cost of Attendance) of $54,180, that amounts to a 56% discount. This figure is close to Harvey Mudd's (56%), Macalester (55%), and more than big school such as Northwestern (48%).

For career, according to www.payscale.com, Carleton graduates earn an average "mid-career" salary of $105,000, beating all UC Schools except for UC-Berkeley. This figure also trounced Mid-west rivals such as Northwestern ($91,900), Macalester ($84,600), Washington Univ. - St. Louis ($91,400).

As for Ph.D. rate, Carleton ranked 6th in all of U.S. for its graduates obtaining math/science Ph.D. later on. With an 11.7% rate, Carleton is even ranked above top-ranked schools (according to *U.S. News*) such as Univ. of Chicago (10.8%), and HYPS (Harvard/Yale/Princeton/Stanford). These figures are according to Nat'l Science Foundation. All these factors lead us to conclude Carleton is "generous" in terms of financial aid and career prospects.

Ethnicity & Leverage

Asians have excellent leverage when applying to Carleton. As seen on Chart A, Whites outnumber Asian 11-to-1 (68% vs. 6%). A school of Carleton's caliber is certainly seeking to recruit top Asian students. If your test scores are at 75 percentile (Chart C), you are like to gain admission with *above average* financial aid offer. Even if your scores are at the 50 percentile range, you still have a good chance of getting in (especially Male Asian).

Athletics

If we add sports as an additional factor, Asian student-athletes would be in high demand at Carleton (assuming you are a good student). However, we believe Asian ethnicity is big enough of a factor already.

You Can Study Science as well as Liberal Arts

As seen clearly in Chart E, 35% Carleton students major in math/science, which is more than "universities" such as Northwestern (25%), U of Chicago (22%), and Washington U-St. Louis (28%). Thus, you can study "arts and science" at Carleton. Indeed, the top 2 majors at Carleton are biology (12%) and physical science (12%). As for non-math/science majors, Economics (7%) lead the way.

Conclusion

In summary, the following "secrets" will increase your chances significantly at Carleton for admissions and more financial aid:

1) Asian students are "underrepresented" at Carleton (only 4%);
2) Be male;
3) Apply to all majors. CA students have "geographic" advantage;
4) No need to apply Early Decision because Asians have leverage;
5) Student-athlete.

Macalester College

A) Ethnicity

White	Asian	Race Unknown	Int'l Students
69%	6%	0%	11%

B) Admission Rates

Overall Admit Rate	Regular Admit Rate	Early Action/Early Decision
34.8%	NA	NA

C) Test Scores

SAT	**25 Percentile**	**75 Percentile**
Reading	640	740
Math	620	710
Writing	630	730
ACT	28	32

D) Financial Aid

% 1st Yr Student Receiving Grants	Avg Grants 1st Yr Student	Total Cost of Attendance (COA)
75%	$30,021	$54,277

E) Majors and Fields of Study

% Degrees in Math, Sci/Engr	Degrees in Other
22%	78%

Macalester College

Perhaps "unknown" to many Asian students and parents, Macalester is conveniently located just 6 miles from the St. Paul/Minneapolis Int'l Airport, a hub for many flight in the U.S. As a small "liberal arts" school, it is naturally a peer (and rival) of Carleton, which is 40 miles away. With an undergrad enrollment of 2,000, it is 58% female and 42% male. Macalester is ranked 26th by *U.S. News* for liberal arts.

Money Matters & Career

A whopping 75% of Macalester freshmen students receive an average grant of $30,021. Macaelster's 75% figures is the highest of any school (Carleton =52%) profiled in this book. Yes, it is higher than Harvard (57%) or Yale (51%). Please see their respective sections. And each Macalester recipient receives "quite a bundle" (i.e. $30K). Against a total COA (Cost of Attendance) of $54,277, that amounts to a 55% discount for Macalester. This 55% discount is the same as Carleton (56%).

For career, according to www.payscale.com, Macalester graduates earn an average "mid-career" salary of $84,600 (vs. $105K for Carleton). While this $84.6K can be viewed as a bit low, it is the same as Wellesley ($84.6K). Overall, Macalester's salary trails behind other Mid-west rivals such as Northwestern ($91,900), Macalester ($84,600), Washington U-St. Louis ($91,400).

As for Ph.D. rate, Macalester ranked 28th (7.1%) in all of U.S. for its graduates obtaining math/science Ph.D. later on. Macalester's 7.1% rate (Carleton=11.7%) is even ranked above top-ranked national universities (according to *U.S. News*) such as Univ. of Duke (6.8%), UC-Berkeley (5.7%) and Dartmouth (5.7%). Its mid-west rivals Northwestern and Washington U-St. Louis did not even make the top 50. These figures are according to Nat'l Science Foundation. Thus, although average mid-career is on the low side, the "wide-spread" (75% of 1st year students) financial aid and high rate of Ph.D. makes Macalester a generous school.

Ethnicity & Leverage

Just like Carleton, Asian has leverage when applying to Macalester. Asians are only at 6% in Macalester (same as Carleton). Interestingly, Macalester has 11% International students, *more* than Asian-Americans. Again, we believe Macalester is looking to attract top Asian students. Thus, If your test scores are at 75 percentile (Chart C), you are like to gain admission with *above average* financial aid offer. Even if your scores are at the 50 percentile range, you still have a good chance of getting in (especially for Male Asians).

You Can Study Science as well as Liberal Arts

As seen clearly in Chart E, many Macalester student math/science (22%). Thus, you can study "arts and science" at Macalester. Indeed, the top 2 majors at Macalester are biology (12%) and physical science (12%). As for non-math/science majors, Economics (7%) lead the way.

Athletics

If we add sports as an additional factor, Asian student-athletes would be in high demand at Macalester (assuming you are a good student). However, we believe Asian ethnicity is big enough of a factor already.

Conclusion

In summary, the following "secrets" will increase your chances significantly at Macalester for admissions and more financial aid:

1) Asian students are "underrepresented" at Macalester (only 6%);
2) Be male;
3) Apply to all majors. CA students have "geographic" advantage;
4) No need to apply Early Decision because Asians have leverage;
5) Student-athlete.

Carnegie Mellon University

A) Ethnicity

White	Asian	Race Unknown	Int'l Students
42%	22%	7%	6%

B) Admission Rates

Overall Admit Rate	Regular Admit Rate	Early Action/Early Decision
27.1%	27.0%	26.0%

C) Test Scores

SAT	**25 Percentile**	**75 Percentile**
Reading	620	720
Math	680	780
Writing	630	730
ACT	29	33

D) Financial Aid

% 1st Yr Student Receiving Grants	Avg Grants 1st Yr Student	Total Cost of Attendance (COA)
51%	$24,680	$57,520

E) Majors and Fields of Study

% Degrees in Math, Sci/Engr	Degrees in Other
57%	43%

Carnegie Mellon University

Carnegie Mellon ("CMU") is a premier science and engineering school. Located in Pittsburg, Pennsylvania, it is ranked 23rd according to the latest *U.S. News & World* Report college rankings.

Money Matters & Career

51% of Carnegie Mellon freshmen students receive an average grant of $24,680. Against a total COA (Cost of Attendance) of $57,520, that amounts to a 43% discount for Carnegie Mellon. This "discount" falls below Case Western (46%) and Northwestern (48%). That only 51% of CMU 1st year student receive grants also falls behind Case Western.

For career, according to www.payscale.com, CMU graduates earn an average "mid-career" salary of $108K (vs. $98.6K). This $108K amount by CMU beats all UC schools except UC-Berkeley. Moreover, CMU is right behind Yale ($110K) & UPenn ($111K). It out-distances other Mid-west rivals such as Northwestern ($91,900) and Washington U-St. Louis ($91,400). These factors show that CMU holds its ranking quite well.

Not surprisingly, Carnegie students have a high Ph.D. rate. In fact, CMU ranked 27th (close to its *U.S. News Report* ranking) in all of U.S. for its graduates obtaining math/science Ph.D. later on. (Actually, CMU is tied with Macalester). Thus, Carnegie Mellon's 7.1% rate is even ranked above top-ranked national universities (according to *U.S. News*) such as Univ. of Duke (6.8%), UC-Berkeley (5.7%) and Dartmouth (5.7%). Its mid-west rivals Northwestern and Washington U-St. Louis did not even make the top 50. These figures are according to Nat'l Science Foundation.

Thus, although financial aid discount is a bit low, the high mid-career salary and high rate of Ph.D. makes Carnegie Mellon a generous school.

Ethnicity & Leverage

CMU is popular among Asians students. Chart A shows that Whites outnumber Asian by almost 2-to-1 (42% vs. 22%). Thus, Asians do not have as much leverage as other schools profiled in this book. However, Asian female applicants should still enjoy more leverage because CMU has 58% male. For male Asian applicants, you would need to be close to the 75 percentile in test scores (Chart C) to have a sure chance of admission. For CA applicants, those numbers can be less because CMU has mostly students from East Coast.

Athletics

Sports would be a big factor because CMU sports teams are *not* in Division I (e.g. Notre Dame/Duke/Stanford). Since Asians do not have too much leverage otherwise, athletics would boost a student's (especially male Asian) application.

You Can Study Science as well as Liberal Arts

As seen clearly in Chart E, CMU is balanced between science/engineering and other areas of study. The most popular major at CMU is Engineering (29%), with Computer Science (12%) a distant second. As for Biology, it is at 5.6%. Even for a technical school such as CMU, only 4% students study Math. Among non- science/engineering majors, Business (10%) leads the way. As mentioned, CMU student also have a high rate of obtaining Ph.D. subsequently.

Conclusion

In summary, the following "secrets" will increase your chances significantly at Carnegie Mellon for admissions:

1) Do NOT apply for Early Decision since admit rate is **lower**;
2) Be female (male=58% at Carnegie Mellon);
3) CA students have "geographic" advantage;
4) Student-athlete.

Case Western University

A) Ethnicity

White	Asian	Race Unknown	Int'l Students
55%	16%	14%	6%

B) Admission Rates

Male Admit Rate	Female Admit Rate	Overall Admit Rate
67.1%	66.2%	66.7%

C) Test Scores

SAT	**25 Percentile**	**75 Percentile**
Reading	600	700
Math	650	750
Writing	590	700
ACT	28	32

D) Financial Aid

% 1st Yr Student Receiving Grants	Avg Grants 1st Yr Student	Total Cost of Attendance (COA)
65%	$25,342	$54,585

E) Majors and Fields of Study

% Degrees in Math, Sci/Engr	Degrees in Other
54%	46%

Case Western University ("CW")

Located in Cleveland, Case Western's specialty is science and engineering. According to the latest *U.S. News & World* Report college rankings, Case Western is ranked 41st, tied with UC-Irvine and RPI (Rensselaer Institute of Technology).

Money Matters & Career

65% of CW freshmen students receive an average grant of $25,342. Against a total COA (Cost of Attendance) of $54,585, that amounts to a 46% discount for Case Western. This discount bests Carnegie Mellon's (43%) but falls behind Northwestern (48%). Case Western's 65% ratio for 1st year students receiving grants (Chart C) is the highest of any Mid-west Elite schools profiled here.

For career, according to www.payscale.com, Case Western graduates can expect an impressive $98.6K of "mid-career" (15 years experience) salary. This puts CW right behind USC ($99.4K), although USC is ranked 23rd by *U.S. News*. Against other mid-western rivals, CW falls short against Carnegie Mellon ($108K) and Notre Dame ($112K). However, CW's salary figure surprisingly defeats Northwestern ($91.9K) and Washington U-St. Louis ($91.4K). We say "surprisingly" because NW and Washington U-St. Louis are ranked 12th and 13th, respectively by *U.S. News*. Thus, by outperforming higher ranked rivals, CW should move up the rankings.

As for Ph.D. rate, CW also scored well, ranking 23rd, according to the Nat'l Science Foundation. CW students will likely obtain Ph.D. subsequently at a rate of 7.5%, just in front of Carnegie Mellon (7.1%). CW's Ph.D. rate is also ahead of UC-Berkeley (5.7%). Thus, based all these factors, we can conclude CW is generous.

Ethnicity & Leverage

Chart B shows that CW's has a very high acceptance rate (2 out of 3 applicants are admitted, the highest of any school profiled in this book). Thus, we don't believe you need other factors if your test scores at 50 percentile. If you are female (CW has 58% male) or from CA, then you probably can get in with 25 percentile test scores. But the ease of admission does not mean CW's education is substandard. As shown above, CW graduates can expect a high salary and high Ph.D. rate.

Thus, with possible high salary and Ph.D. rate, we wonder why students just "ignore" CW and apply to schools that have much lower acceptance rates (i.e. Northwestern, Johns Hopkins, Washington U-St. Louis). No wonder CW's website states CW is "under the radar."

Our observation for parents and students from CA is as follows: either attend H/Y/P and nothing else. However, the average acceptance rate for Harvard, Yale and Princeton = 7% (i.e. there is a **93% failure rate**). So that type of approach thinking fails 93 percent of time, which totally ignores fine schools like Case Western. Thus, at the very least, CW should be a safety school. With 66% acceptance rate, CA students would be welcomed at CW. Furthermore, if you are going to apply to Carnegie Mellon, CW should be a worthy "back-up" because all of the above positive factors.

You Can Study Science as well as Liberal Arts

As seen clearly in Chart E, Case Western is balanced between science/engineering (54%) and other areas of study (46%). Not surprisingly, the most popular majors are Engineering (27%) and Biology (12%). As a comparison, 29% Carnegie Mellon's students study Engineering and 5.6% study Biology. Among non- science/engineering majors, Business (10.5%) leads the way, same as Carnegie Mellon. As mentioned, Case Western students also have a high rate of obtaining Ph.D. subsequently.

Conclusion

In summary, the following strategies will increase your chances at Case Western:

1) Actually, there isn't any secrets – just apply;
2) High acceptance rate (2/3 get in) = "Safety School";
3) Asian/International students have leverage;
4) Female has even more leverage since CW has 56% male;
5) CA students have "geographic" advantage.

CONFERENCE SEVEN: Select UC Schools

UC Schools do provide financial aid. So we want to see what they compare to private schools. We picked the 6 UC schools that most Asian students would apply. Furthermore, we also included Cal-Poly San Luis Obispo for its low admission rate and its reputation for science and engineering. The financial aid comparison is as follows:

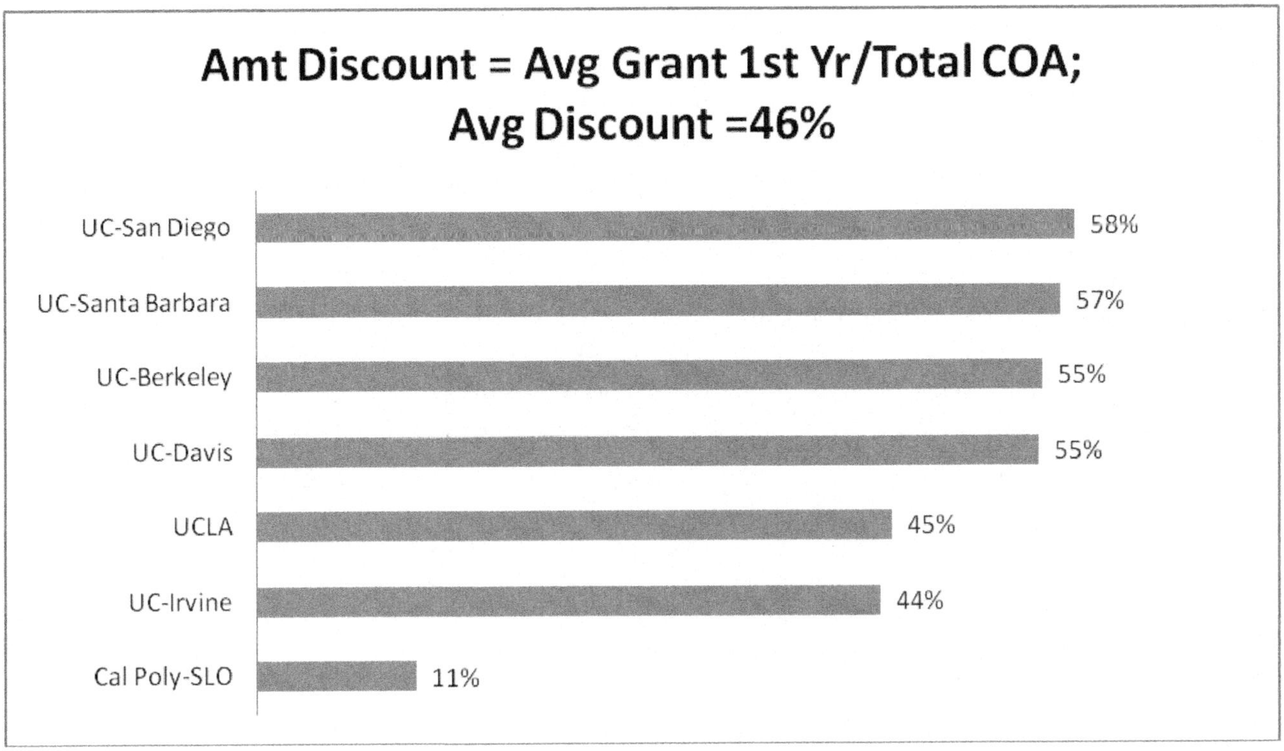

Thus, the Chart shows that financial aid for UC is different from school to school. The most generous is UC-San Diego, followed closely by UC-Santa Barbara. And there is a big difference between UCLA and UC-Berkeley's discount. Some of the data numbers here will surprise many readers.

We are profiling this Conference in this order:

Select UC Schools:

UC-Berkeley
UCLA
UC-San Diego
UC-Irvine
UC-Davis
UC-Santa Barbara
Cal Poly- San Luis Obispo

UC-Berkeley

A) Ethnicity

White	Asian	Race Unknown	Int'l Students
30%	40%	7%	7%

B) Admission Rates

Overall Admit Rate	Regular Admit Rate	Early Action/Early Decision
21.1%	21.1%	No EA/ED Program

C) Test Scores

SAT	**25 Percentile**	**75 Percentile**
Reading	600	730
Math	630	760
Writing	610	740
ACT	27	33

D) Financial Aid

% 1st Yr Student Receiving Grants	Avg Grants 1st Yr Student	Total Cost of Attendance (COA)
56%	$17,468	$31,566

E) Majors and Fields of Study

% Degrees in Math, Sci/Engr	Degrees in Other
31%	69%

UC-Berkeley

UC-Berkeley is the viewed by many as the top UC school. Indeed, *U.S. News* ranks it at No. 21, ahead of UCLA (25th). Renowned for high academics and famous professors in the faculty ranks, Berkeley attracts many high achieving CA students. However, Berkeley students do not think of UCLA as a competitor. Actually, Berkeley's greatest rival is Stanford (ranked 5th). Berkeley measures practially everything against Stanford.

Financial Aid & Career Prospects

46% of UC-Berkeley's 1st year students receive an average grant of $17,468. (Please see Chart D). Against the total Cost of Attendance (COA) of $31,566, that represents a 55% discount off the sticker price. Berkeley's discount beats private schools such as Univ. of Chiago (48%), Northwestern (48%), Georgetown (48%), Johns Hopkins (48%), and Washington U-St. Louis (41%).

Furthermore, according to *U.S. News,* all these private schools are ranked above Berkeley. Thus, despite the budget crisis affecting UC Schools, Berkeley still manage to offer a great discount to those students who qualified. Against its bitter rival Stanford, Berkeley's discount falls short (Stanford's discount = 66%).

As for mid-career salary (15 years experience), Berkeley graduates report an average of $109K, the highest among UC Schools. This is according to www.payscale.com. Berkeley's $109K is right behind Ivy Leaguers UPenn ($111K), Yale ($110K) and tied with Brown ($109K). Thus, it is clear than Berkeley's education and salary is comparable to the Ivy League. Furthermore, Berkeley's salary figure also overwhelmed higher ranking private schools like Johns Hopkins ($90K), Northwestern ($92K), and Washington U-St. Louis ($91.4K). Against Stanford, it is about 9% short (Stanford's salary = $119K). Nevertheless, Berkeley's salary figure held up its ranking (21st) very well. Based on the salary figures, perhaps Berkeley should move up the *U.S. News* rankings.

Berkeley, as expected, also score well in the Ph. D. rate category. According to the National Science Foundation, Berkeley is ranked 39th among all schools whose graduates is likely to obtain Ph.D.'s in science/engineering subsequently. Indeed, Berkeley's 5.7% rate is highest among all UC schools and tied with Dartmouth. Stanford has an 8.1% rate. But still Berkeley held up its ranking here as well. These figures are according to the Nat'l Science Foundation.

Overall, due to Berkeley's high discount (for a public school), excellent mid-career salary, and high Ph.D. rate, we conclude UC-Berkeley is a generous school.

Ethnicity & Leverage?

Chart A clearly shows Asians outnumber Whites in Berkeley (40% vs. 30%). In fact, Asian is the largest ethnic group at Berkeley (and in several other UC schools also). Thus, it is clear that Asians have no leverage when applying to UC-Berkeley (this is probably a fact that many people are aware of).

So what are some ways you can at least increase your chances? It would have to be based on choosing a major. As discussed in the section regarding Math, there are not enough students choosing math as a major in general. Berkeley is no exception, with only 3% student studying. As we also discussed in the section on Math, more Asian students should study it because they are strong AND math serve a excellent fundamental subject to be used as a springboard for graduate school and jobs. Thus, for those Asian applicants who are strong in math and wish to gain acceptance into Berkeley, they should apply Math as major.

Sports Any Help for Berkeley?

Not likely. This is because Berkeley teams compete in Div. I (highest level). Berkeley has very strong athletic tradition in football, baseball and basketball. This past spring, its swimming teams (men's and women's) both won the NCAA Division I Championships, beating arch-rival Stanford in the process. But the point here is that sports would help only if your skills are at "college champion" level.

Study Science/Engineering and Liberal Arts

While Berkeley is known for science an
d engineering, Chart E shows that almost 70% of Berkeley students study other areas. The most popular majors are Engineering (12%) and Biology (12%). The numbers for Math (3%) and Physics (less than 1%) are low. As for non-science/engineering majors, Economics (6%), Political Science (5%), and English (5%) lead the way.

Conclusion

In summary, the following strategies will increase your UC-Berkeley chances and perhaps your financial aid offer;

1) Ethnicity = Unknown;
2) Be male (Berkeley = 53% female);
3) Apply for math major if you are interested;
4) Try to avoid "hot" majors like biology;
5) Student-Athlete probably would not help unless recruited.

UCLA

A) Ethnicity

White	Asian	Race Unknown	Int'l Students
32%	36%	4%	6%

B) Admission Rates

Overall Admit Rate	Regular Admit Rate	Early Action/Early Decision
21.1%	21.1%	No EA/ED Program

C) Test Scores

SAT	**25 Percentile**	**75 Percentile**
Reading	570	680
Math	600	760
Writing	610	740
ACT	27	33

D) Financial Aid

% 1st Yr Student Receiving Grants	Avg Grants 1st Yr Student	Total Cost of Attendance (COA)
59%	$13,643	$30,577

E) Majors and Fields of Study

% Degrees in Math, Sci/Engr	Degrees in Other
27%	73%

UCLA

Most CA students usually have either UCLA or UC-Berkeley as their No. 1 choice. Ranked No. 25th by U.S. News, it is just a few notches below UC-Berkeley and ahead of rest of the UC schools. Although UC-Berkeley is certainly a rival, UCLA students have an intense rivalry (and dislike) for cross-town rival USC. With an enrollment of 26,000, the females/male split for UCLA is 55% vs. 45%.

Financial Aid & Career Prospects

47% of UCLA's 1st year students receive an average grant of $13,643. (Please see Chart D). Against the total Cost of Attendance (COA) of $30,577, that represents only a 45% discount off the sticker price. This 45% discount is tied with UCI (44%) for the lowest among the UC Schools we are profiling. For example, UC-Berkeley (55%), UC-Santa Barbara (57%) and UC-San Diego (58%) all beat UCLA's discount. Thus, we can clearly see that a student do NOT receive the same financial aid from different UC schools. However, UCLA's 45% discount is the same against USC (45%).

As for mid-career salary (15 years experience), UCLA graduates report an average of $91.6K. This is according to www.payscale.com. Thus, UCLA's $91.6K falls behind UC-Berkeley's ($109K), UC- San Diego ($99.7K), and even Cal Poly-SLO ($99.2K). UCLA's salary figure does beat UC-Irvine ($92.5K) and UC-Davis ($90.7K).

Furthermore, the UCLA salary figure is lower than USC, who reported $99.4K. This has to hurt as USC beat UCLA on the *U.S. News* rankings for the first time with a ranking of 23rd. Furthermore, USC has been winning the annual football game against UCLA on a regular basis. Thus, almost everything UCLA does is measured against USC, the way UC-Berkeley is measured against Stanford.

UCLA is not ranked in the top-50 schools whose graduates is likely to obtain Ph.D.'s in science/engineering subsequently. Neither is USC. UC-Berkeley, on the other hand, is ranked 39th with a 5.7% rate. These numbers are according to the National Science Foundation.

Now we do understand that UC schools are facing a budget crunch. However, if other UC schools are able to offer a bigger discount, then why not UCLA? Furthermore, in times of budget cutbacks, the amount of discount become an even more important factor. Thus, with a lower discount and a not-so-high salary number, we conclude UCLA is not as generous as other schools.

Ethnicity & Leverage?

Chart A clearly shows Asians outnumber Whites in UCLA (36% vs. 32%). Thus, the joke that UCLA means "University of Caucasian Lost among Asians" may indeed be an accurate description. Thus, Asian has no leverage when applying to UCLA. So what can Asian applicant do to increase chances?

Sports is NOT an option because UCLA competes in Division I's Pacific-12 Conference (along with UC-Berkeley, Stanford, and USC). Thus, above average athletes would *not* have an impact on admissions at all. Thus, just like UC-Berkeley, the "side door" into UCLA is to apply for the "right" major. Read on.

Study Science/Engineering and Liberal Arts

Chart E shows that almost 27% of UCLA students study math, science and engineering. As many of you know, Biology is the hottest major in science currently. On the other end of the spectrum there are Math and Physics, which many Asian students view as "uncool" even though they are strong students. (Please see our Special Section on Math vs. Business).

We believe Math is an excellent fundamental major. Thus, we suggest you apply Math or Physics as major UCLA. Furthermore, in the first 2 years, Math and Physics majors take many science course as requirements anyway. Thus, if you don't like Math as a major, you can transfer into Biology without missing a beat because you have been taking science courses all along. This "roadmap" would be easier to you to gain acceptance into UCLA. If an Asian student applies for Biology straight from high school, there is a very high chance of rejection (i.e. around 80%; see Chart A.)

So let's look at the numbers. Biology and related major is the single most popular science/engr. major in UCLA (14%). Engineering is a distant second (7.6%). As expected, the percentage of UCLA students studying Math (2.7%) and Physics (1.65%) are low. Among non-science/engineering majors, Psychology (10%) and Political Science (7.6%) are tops. These numbers are complied by the Nat'l Center for Education Statistics, as reported by UCLA.

Conclusion

In summary, the following "strategies" will increase your UCLA chances and perhaps your financial aid offer;

1) Ethnicity = Unknown;
2) Be male (UCLA = 55% female);
3) Major = Math or Physics;
4) Try to avoid "hot" majors like biology;
5) Student-Athlete probably would not help unless recruited.

UC- San Diego ("UCSD")

A) Ethnicity

White	Asian	Race Unknown	Int'l Students
24%	44%	10%	7%

B) Admission Rates

Overall Admit Rate	Regular Admit Rate	Early Action/Early Decision
37.1%	37.1%	No EA/ED Program

C) Test Scores

SAT	**25 Percentile**	**75 Percentile**
Reading	540	670
Math	610	720
Writing	560	690
ACT	25	31

D) Financial Aid

% 1st Yr Student Receiving Grants	Avg Grants 1st Yr Student	Total Cost of Attendance (COA)
64%	$16,309	$28,275

E) Majors and Fields of Study

% Degrees in Math, Sci/Engr	Degrees in Other
40%	60%

UC-San Diego ("UCSD")

Ranked 35th by the latest *U.S. News* College Rankings, UCSD is the 3rd highest among UC Schools, behind UC-Berkeley and UCLA. Like other UC's, it has a large undergrad population of 23,600. Ranked right behind trendy private school NYU, UCSD has a female-male split at 49% male and 51% female.

Financial Aid & Career Prospects

64% of UCSD's 1st year students receive an average grant of $16,309. (Please see Chart D). Against the total Cost of Attendance (COA) of $28,275, that represents only a 58% discount off the sticker price. This 58% discount is the highest among all UC schools. Thus, we can clearly see that a student do NOT receive the same financial aid from different UC schools.

As for mid-career salary (15 years experience), UCSD graduates report an average of $91.6K. This is according to www.payscale.com. Thus, UCSD's $91.6K falls behind UC-Berkeley's ($109K), UC- San Diego ($99.7K), and even Cal Poly-SLO ($99.2K). UCSD's salary figure does beat UC-Irvine ($92.5K) and UC-Davis ($90.7K). Against private schools ranked near itself, UCSD's salary number falters against Carnegie Mellon ($108K), Tufts ($96.4K) and Univ. of Virginia ($93.9K).

UCSD is not ranked in the top-50 schools whose graduates is likely to obtain Ph.D.'s in science/engineering subsequently. Neither is USC. UC-Berkeley, on the other hand, is ranked 39th with a 5.7% rate. These numbers are according to the National Science Foundation.

Overall, with a *highest* discount in the UC system, and a respectable salary number, we conclude UCSD is as a generous school.

Ethnicity & Leverage?

Chart A clearly shows Asians outnumber White in UCSD (44% vs. 24%). Thus, Asian has *no leverage* when applying to UCSD.

For Sports, UCSD play in Division II, which do not offer athletic scholarship but does recruit athletes. Thus, student-athletes can use sports as leverage into UCSD, since the athletic skills required as not as high as Stanford or USC.

Study Science/Engineering and Liberal Arts

Chart E shows that almost 40% of UCSD students study math, science and engineering. As many of you know, Biology is the hottest major in science currently. On the other end of the spectrum there are Math and Physics, which many Asian students view as "uncool" even though they are strong students. (Please see our Special Section on Math vs. Business).

We believe Math is an excellent fundamental major. Thus, we suggest you apply Math or Physics as major UCSD. Furthermore, in the first 2 years, Math and Physics majors take many science course as requirements anyway. Thus, if you don't like Math as a major, you can transfer into Biology without missing a beat because you have been taking science courses all along. This "roadmap" would be easier to you to gain acceptance into UCSD.

So let's look at the numbers. Biology and related major is the single most popular overall in UCSD (22%). Engineering lags far behind at 11%. As expected, the percentage of UCSD students studying Math (2%) and Physics (3.7%) are low. Among non-science/engineering majors, Economics (9%) and Psychology (8%) are tops. These numbers are complied by the Nat'l Center for Education Statistics, as reported by UCSD.

In summary, these numbers clearly show that Math and Physics students are less than those in Biology, and thus help support our above strategy.

Conclusion

In summary, the following "strategies" will increase your UCSD chances and perhaps your financial aid offer;

1) Ethnicity = Unknown;
2) Be male (UCSD = 51% female);
3) Major = Math or Physics;
4) Try to avoid "hot" majors like biology;
5) Student-Athlete probably would not help unless recruited.

UC-Irvine ("UCI")

A) Ethnicity

White	Asian	Race Unknown	Int'l Students
22%	53%	6%	3%

B) Admission Rates

Overall Admit Rate	Regular Admit Rate	Early Action/Early Decision
36.3%	36.3%	No EA/ED Program

C) Test Scores

SAT	**25 Percentile**	**75 Percentile**
Reading	524	640
Math	570	680
Writing	530	640
ACT	No data	No data

D) Financial Aid

% 1st Yr Student Receiving Grants	Avg Grants 1st Yr Student	Total Cost of Attendance (COA)
52%	$12,406	$28,357

E) Majors and Fields of Study

% Degrees in Math, Sci/Engr	Degrees in Other
31%	69%

UC-Irvine ("UCI")

Ranked 41st by the latest *U.S. News* College Rankings, UC-Irvine ("UCI") has become a sought after school for CA students of all ethnicities. Like other UC's, it has a large undergrad population of 23,600. Its male-female split is fairly even at 47% male and 53% female.

Financial Aid & Career Prospects

50% of UCI's 1st year students receive an average grant of $12,406. (Please see Chart D). Against the total Cost of Attendance (COA) of $28,357, that represents only a 44% discount off the sticker price. This 44% discount is the *lowest* among the UC schools we are profiling.

As for mid-career salary (15 years experience), UCI graduates report an average of $92.5K. This is according to www.payscale.com. Thus, UCI's $92.5K falls behind UC-Berkeley's ($109K), UC-San Diego ($99.7K), and even Cal Poly-SLO ($99.2K). UCI's salary number does *beat* several private schools ranked above, namely Northwestern (12th/$91.9K), Johns Hopkins (13th/$90.1K), and Washington Univ.-St. Louis (13th/$91.4K).

UCI is not ranked in the top-50 schools whose graduates is likely to obtain Ph.D.'s in science/engineering subsequently. Again, only Berkeley is the only UC on the list. These rankings are according to the National Science Foundation.

Overall, while UCI has a discount that is lower than other UC's, it has a very respectable mid-career salary figure, beating several private schools ranked above them. We also have to consider the fact that as a state school, it is facing a huge funding short-fall. Thus, we conclude UCI is a generous school.

Ethnicity & Leverage?

Chart A clearly shows Asians outnumber White in UCI by *more than 2-to-1.* (53% vs. 22%). This is the only major school we know with such wide disparity. Thus, Asians has *no leverage* at when applying to UCI.

Sports is NOT an option because UCI competes in Division I (most competitive). Although UCI does not yet have the athletic tradition of USC or Stanford, it does provide athletic scholarships. Thus, above average athletes would not have an impact on admissions at all. With an excellent sports tradition, UCI is looking for top-level athletes. Thus, the "road map" into UCI for Asian applicants would be choosing the "right" major.

Study Science/Engineering and Liberal Arts

Chart E shows that almost 31% of UCI students study math, science and engineering. As expected, the most popular major is Biology and related (16%) and Engineering is next at 8%. Math (1%) and Computer Science (2.5%) are low and are "screaming" for more students.

Among non-science/engineering majors, Business (7.5%) and Psychology (6%) lead the way.

Conclusion

In summary, the following strategies will increase your UCI chances and perhaps your financial aid offer;

1) Ethnicity = Unknown;
2) Female has higher admit rate;
3) Major = Math, Computer Science or Physics;
4) Try to avoid "hot" majors like biology;
5) Student-Athlete probably would not help unless recruited.

UC- Davis

A) Ethnicity

White	Asian	Race Unknown	Int'l Students
34%	38%	5%	2%

B) Admission Rates

Overall Admit Rate	Regular Admit Rate	Early Action/Early Decision
47.7%	47.7%	No EA/ED Program

C) Test Scores

SAT	**25 Percentile**	**75 Percentile**
Reading	530	650
Math	570	690
Writing	540	660
ACT	24	30

D) Financial Aid

% 1st Yr Student Receiving Grants	Avg Grants 1st Yr Student	Total Cost of Attendance (COA)
63%	$16,105	$29,259

E) Majors and Fields of Study

% Degrees in Math, Sci/Engr	Degrees in Other
44%	56%

UC-Davis ("UCD")

Ranked 39th by the latest *U.S. News* College Rankings, UC-Davis is located near Sacramento with an undergrad enrollment of approximately 25,000. Actually, it is tied with UC-Santa Barbara for the 39th place ranking. UCD's male-female split is at 45% male and 55% female.

Financial Aid & Career Prospects

63% of UCD's 1st year students receive an average grant of $16,105. (Please see Chart D). Against the total Cost of Attendance (COA) of $29,259, that represents a 55% discount off the sticker price. The number of 1st-year student receiving grants at UC-Davis (63%) is the highest with UC-San Diego among UC schools.

As for mid-career salary (15 years experience), UCD graduates report an average of $90.7K. This is according to www.payscale.com. This salary number is very respectable because it beats such fine schools such as Univ. of Michigan (ranked 29th/$90.2K), Johns Hopkins (ranked 13th/$90.1K), Emory (ranked 20th/$90K), and NYU (ranked 33rd/$88.8K).

Despite its science/engineering emphasis (44%; see Chart E), UC-Davis is not among the top-50 schools whose graduates obtain Ph.D. in science and engineering. This is according to National Science Foundation.

Overall, with a reasonable discount and respectable mid-career salary number, we conclude UCD is a generous school.

Ethnicity & Leverage?

Chart A clearly shows Asians outnumber White in UCD (38% vs. 34%). And since UCD emphasizes science and engineering, areas of study that is popular among Asians, UCD would be even harder for Asians to get in. Thus, what type of "leverage" does Asians have?

Sports is mostly not an option because UCD competes in Division I (most competitive). Although UCD is not at the athletic level of Stanford and USC, most of UC-Davis' teams are looking for "high level" athletes. Then we are down to picking majors as the last possible leverage left.

Study Science/Engineering and Liberal Arts

Chart E shows that almost 44% of UCD students study math, science and engineering. Not surprisingly, Biology & related majors is the most popular at 22%. Engineering is a distant second (8%). Among non-science/engineering majors, Psychology (10%) and Economics (6%) are tops.

Conclusion

In summary, the following "strategies" will increase your UCD chances and perhaps your financial aid offer;

1) Ethnicity = Unknown;
2) Be male (UCD = 55% female);
3) Major = Math or Physics;
4) Try to avoid "hot" majors like biology;
5) Student-Athlete probably would not help unless recruited.

UC- Santa Barbara ("UCSB")

A) Ethnicity

White	Asian	Race Unknown	Int'l Students
39%	14%	5%	1%

B) Admission Rates

Overall Admit Rate	Regular Admit Rate	Early Action/Early Decision
42.3%	42.3%	No EA/ED Program

C) Test Scores

SAT	**25 Percentile**	**75 Percentile**
Reading	540	650
Math	560	680
Writing	540	660
ACT	25	30

D) Financial Aid

% 1st Yr Student Receiving Grants	Avg Grants 1st Yr Student	Total Cost of Attendance (COA)
55%	$15,718	$27,746

E) Majors and Fields of Study

% Degrees in Math, Sci/Engr	Degrees in Other
17%	83%

UC-Santa Barbara ("UCSB")

UC-Santa Barbara ranked for 39th (tied with UC-Davis) in the latest *U.S. News* College Rankings. With a smaller enrollment (19,000) than most other UC schools, UCSB's female-male split is at 53% female and 47% male.

Financial Aid & Career Prospects

55% of UCSB's 1st year students receive an average grant of $15,718. (Please see Chart D). Against the total Cost of Attendance (COA) of $27,746, that represents a 57% discount off the sticker price. The number of 1st-year student receiving grants at UC-Santa Barbara (63%) is the highest with UC-San Diego among UC schools.

As for mid-career salary (15 years experience), UCSB graduates report an average of $90.7K. This is according to www.payscale.com. This salary number is very respectable because it beats such fine schools such as Univ. of Michigan (ranked 29th/$90.2K), Johns Hopkins (ranked 13th/$90.1K), Emory (ranked 20th/$90K), and NYU (ranked 33rd/$88.8K).

Despite its science/engineering emphasis (44%; see Chart E), UC-Santa Barbara is not among the top-50 schools whose graduates obtain Ph.D. in science and engineering. This is according to National Science Foundation.

Overall, with a reasonable discount and respectable mid-career salary number, we conclude UCSB is a generous school.

Ethnicity & Leverage?

Chart A clearly shows Whites outnumber Asians in UCSB by almost 3-to-1 (39% vs. 14%). This white/Asian gap is also the *highest* among UC Schools. Thus, Asian applicants have plenty of leverage when applying to UCSB.

Sports is mostly not an option because UCSB competes in Division I. Although UCSB is not at the athletic level of Stanford and USC, most of UC-Santa Barbara' teams are looking for "high level" athletes.

We believe ethnicity is the biggest factor here, and there is no need to even use sports as leverage for Asian applicants.

Study Science/Engineering and Liberal Arts

Chart E shows that almost 44% of UCSB students study math, science and engineering. Not surprising, Biology & related majors is the most popular at 22%. Engineering is a distant second (8%). Among non-science/engineering majors, Psychology (10%) and Economics (6%) are tops.

Conclusion

In summary, the following "strategies" will increase your UCSB chances and perhaps your financial aid offer;

1) Ethnicity = Asian;
2) Be male (UCSB = 55% female);
3) Apply to all majors;
4) Student-Athlete probably would not help unless recruited.

Cal Poly – San Luis Obispo

A) Ethnicity

White	Asian	Race Unknown	Int'l Students
65%	10%	7%	1%

B) Admission Rates

Overall Admit Rate	Regular Admit Rate	Early Action/Early Decision
33%	33%	No EA/ED Program

C) Test Scores

SAT	**25 Percentile**	**75 Percentile**
Reading	540	640
Math	580	680
Writing	No data	No data
ACT	24	29

D) Financial Aid

% 1st Yr Student Receiving Grants	Avg Grants 1st Yr Student	Total Cost of Attendance (COA)
24%	$2,394	$21,585

E) Majors and Fields of Study

% Degrees in Math, Sci/Engr	Degrees in Other
32%	68%

Cal Poly – San Luis Obispo

California Polytechnic – San Luis Obispo ("Cal Poly") is part of the California State University system. Ranked No. 6 by the latest *U.S. News* College Rankings for West Regional Universities, Cal Poly is an undiscovered academic gem. Focusing on math, science and engineering, it has an undergrad enrollment of 17,000 (55% female).

Financial Aid & Career Prospects

Only 24% of Cal Poly's 1st year students receive an average grant of $2,394. (Please see Chart D). Against the total Cost of Attendance (COA) of $21,585, that represents only a 11% discount off the sticker price. So why are we even profiling a school with such low discount?

Largely because of its mid-career salary (15 years experience) numbers. Cal Poly graduates report an average of $99.2K. This is according to www.payscale.com. Cal Poly's $99.2K number beats all UC schools except UC-Berkeley ($109K) and UC-San Diego ($99.7K). Yes, Cal Poly beat the much more famous UCLA ($91.6K), and it just missed beating Columbia ($99.7K).

Despite its focus on science and engineering, Cal Poly is not ranked in the top-50 schools whose graduates are likely to obtain a Ph.D. in science or engineering. This is according to the National Science Foundation.

Overall, Cal-Poly is an example of a fine public school (33% admit rate/ Chart B) that provides very little financial aid. A student could obtain more grants from other private schools profiled in this book such that the total "out-the-door" price would be less than Cal Poly's. However, we still conclude Cal Poly-SLO is a generous school due to the high mid-career salary.

Ethnicity & Leverage?

Chart A clearly shows whites outnumber Asian in Cal-Poly by *more than 6-to-1* (65% vs. 10%). This is in *stark contrast* to UC schools where Asians outnumbers whites. Therefore, Asian students would have lots of leverage when applying to Cal-Poly. Frankly, this ratio *shocked* the authors when we first saw it. Here is a state school focusing on engineering and sciences, but it only has 10% Asian. There seems counter-intuitive to us.

We theorize that Asian parents and students think that the Cal State schools are notch below UC's, and thus very few Asian are even thinking of Cal Poly. As we mentioned numerous times, one cannot judge a book by its cover. Cal Poly-SLO has a very high mid-career salary. And Asian students should consider it, especially when Asians has leverage.

Study Science/Engineering and Liberal Arts

Chart E shows that almost 32% of Cal-Poly students study math, science and engineering. As expected, the most popular major is Biology and related (24%) and Engineering is next at 5.5%. Similar to other school, Math (1.2%) and Computer Science (1.5%) are low and are seeking for more students. Among non-science/engineering majors, Business (15%) and Agriculture and related (12%) lead the way.

Conclusion

In summary, the following strategies will increase your Cal-Poly chances and perhaps your financial aid offer;

1) Ethnicity = Asian;
2) Female has slightly higher admit rate;
3) Apply to all majors.

CONFERENCE EIGHT: Southern Elite Schools

Duke is probably the most well-known Southern school to Asian parents and students. We are profiling 5 other excellent schools as well, from smaller Davidson College to Tulane University. The 6 schools offer a average discount of 58% to qualified 1st year students, higher than other conferences profiled such as Select UC and Midwest Elite: The financial aid Chart is as follows:

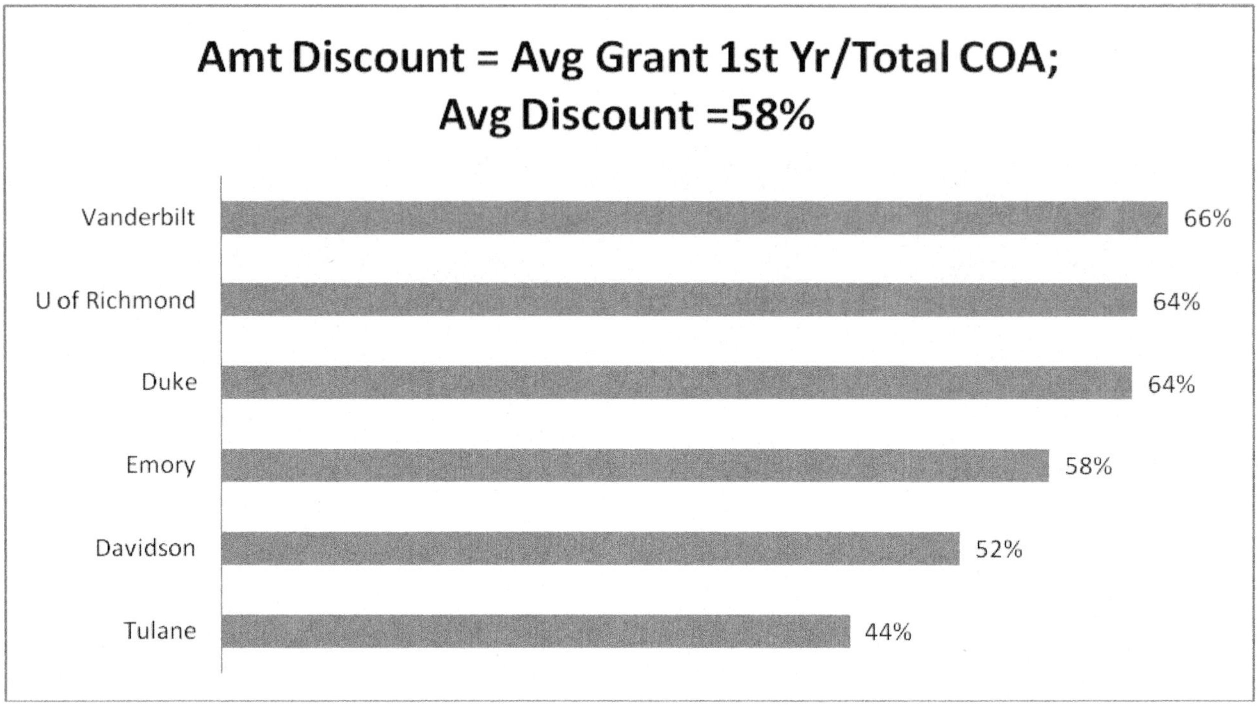

All schools in this Southern Elite offer 50% or more discounts to qualified students, except for Tulane. Vanderbilt (ranked 17th by *U.S. News*) is offering 66%. We believe the more you know about these schools, the more attractive they would become. One thing for sure, these schools are high-caliber as well as generous. We are profiling this Conference in this order:

Southern Elite Schools:

Duke
Vanderbilt
Emory
Tulane
Davidson
Univ. of Richmond

Duke University

A) Ethnicity

White	Asian	Race Unknown	Int'l Students
47%	21%	9%	7%

B) Admission Rates

Overall Admit Rate	Regular Admit Rate	Early Action/Early Decision
11.9%	10.7%	24.5%

C) Test Scores

SAT	**25 Percentile**	**75 Percentile**
Reading	660	750
Math	680	780
Writing	660	760
ACT	30	34

D) Financial Aid

% 1st Yr Student Receiving Grants	Avg Grants 1st Yr Student	Total Cost of Attendance (COA)
51%	$35,440	$55,690

E) Majors and Fields of Study

% Degrees in Math, Sci/Engr	Degrees in Other
31%	69%

Duke University

If you are fortunate to attend Duke, you will be forever blue – as in "Blue Devil", the school's mascot. And you better like (make that love) basketball. Its men's basketball team has been has won the college championship many times. Ranked No. 9 in the latest *U.S. News College Rankings*, Duke combines top academic school with a strong athletic tradition. Located in Durham, North Carolina (only 15 miles from Raleigh Int'l Airport), Duke is perhaps the top school in the South.

Money Matters & Career

51% of Duke 1st year students receive an average grant of $35,440 (Chart D). Against a COA (Cost of Attendance) of $55,690, that amounts to be a 64% discount off the full price. This 64% discount is comparable to the average Ivy League discount of 63%. Furthermore, Duke's 64% just trails Stanford's 66% discount. However, Duke's 64% discount is "head and shoulders" above schools ranked just below, i.e. Univ. of Chicago (48%), Northwestern (48%) and Johns Hopkins (53%).

As for mid-career salary (15 years experience), Duke's graduates scored exceptionally well. Duke's figure of $119K is tied with Stanford, and it trailed narrowly to Harvard ($121K), Princeton ($123K) and Dartmouth ($123K). Against other schools ranked around Duke, it was really no comparison. Specifically, Duke's $119K figure completely overwhelmed Univ. of Chicago ($100K) Northwestern ($91.9K) and Johns Hopkins ($90K). It is almost like these schools basketball teams were playing against Duke's team. All these figures are according to www.payscale.com.

As for Ph.D. rate, Duke is ranked No. 31 (6.8% rate) among schools whose graduates are likely to obtain Ph.D.'s later on. Duke's 6.8% is even ahead of engineering school such as RPI (6.4%). Moreover, Duke's rate is ahead of UC-Berkeley (5.7%) and Dartmouth (5.7%). This is according to National Science Foundation. Based on all these factors, it is clear that Duke is "generous".

Ethnicity & Leverage

Chart A shows Whites outnumber Asians only by 2-to-1 (47% vs. 21%). Since the Asian percentage is already above the Ivy League average of 16%, Asians do not have much average. However, Asian applicants from CA still have geographic advantage.

With that in mind, then Asian students would need test score in the 75 percentile test scores to gain acceptance (Chart C). Sports would be no help unless you are a top, top "recruited" athlete (i.e. many schools fighting over you). As mentioned, Duke's athletic teams all have very strong traditions, especially basketball.

You Can Study Science as well as Liberal Arts

Chart E. shows that plenty of student study science/engineering at Duke (31%). Specifically, 15% study Engineering and 10% study Biology. Among non-science majors, Psychology and Economics are tied with 10%.

Conclusion

In summary, the following "strategies" will increase your chances at Duke:

1) Asians from CA has more leverage;
2) Ethnicity = Unknown/International
3) Apply Early Decision;
4) Apply to math/science/engineering.

Vanderbilt University

A) Ethnicity

White	Asian	Race Unknown	Int'l Students
64%	7%	5%	5%

B) Admission Rates

Overall Admit Rate	Regular Admit Rate	Early Action/Early Decision
13.3%	12.1%	31.2%

C) Test Scores

SAT	**25 Percentile**	**75 Percentile**
Reading	670	760
Math	690	770
Writing	660	750
ACT	30	34

D) Financial Aid

% 1st Yr Student Receiving Grants	Avg Grants 1st Yr Student	Total Cost of Attendance (COA)
44%	$37,174	$56,204

E) Majors and Fields of Study

% Degrees in Math, Sci/Engr	Degrees in Other
31%	69%

Vanderbilt University

A top-20 school (No. 17th by *U.S. News*), Vanderbilt is located in Nashville, Tennessee (self-proclaimed Country Music Capital of U.S.). Despite its high ranking, many Asian students and parents are not familiar with this fine school (Please see Chart A which shows only 7% Asian at Vanderbilt). With undergrad enrollment of approx. has 6,800, Vanderbilt (also nicknamed "Vandy") has a 49/51 male-to-female ratio.

Money Matters & Career

44% of Vandy's 1st-year students receive an average grant of $37,174 (Chart D). Against a COA (Cost of Attendance) of $56,204, that amounts to be a 66% discount off the full price. As a comparison against Southern peers, Vanderbilt's discount beats Duke (64%), Emory (58%) and Tulane (44%). Vandy's discount is also much higher than schools ranked close to it, namely Notre Dame (52%), Rice (53%), and Carnegie Mellon (43%).

For mid-career (15 years experience) salary, Vanderbilt grads report an average of $104K, according to www.payscale.com. This $104K falls behind Duke ($119K), but beats Columbia ($99.7K), Emory ($90K), Rice ($100K) and Tulane ($92.2K). Emory (ranked 20th) and Rice (tied for 17th) are schools that are ranked near Vandy. Thus, Vanderbilt did well in this category for salary.

As for Ph.D. rate, Vanderbilt is not ranked in the top 50 schools whose graduates are likely to obtain Ph.D.'s later on. This is according to Nat'l Science Foundation. However, given all of the above positive factors for Vanderbilt, we conclude it is generous and easily holds up its ranking.

Ethnicity & Leverage

Chart A shows Whites outnumber Asians by 9-to-1 (64% vs. 7%). Thus, we can conclude Vanderbilt would seek to recruit excellent Asian students, and thus Asians would have leverage.

With that in mind, then Asian students would probably need to be around the 50 percentile test scores to gain acceptance (Chart C). If you like an "above average" financial aid offer, then you need to have test scores around 75 percentile.

Sports would be no help unless you are a "recruited" athlete (i.e. wanted badly by the coach), mainly due to the fact that Vandy' teams play in the Divison I's SEC (Southeastern Conference), possibly the best athletic conference in the U.S. As the only private school in the SEC (i.e. higher academic standards), Vandy usually gets "pushed around" by other schools in sports. Thus, Vandy is looking for national level athletes to fight back.

You Can Study Science as well as Liberal Arts

Chart E. shows that plenty of student study science/engineering at Vanderbilt (31%). Specifically, 17% study Engineering and 6.3% study Biology. Among non-science majors, Economics (10%) and Social Science (11%) are the favorites.

Conclusion

In summary, the following "strategies" will increase your chances at Vandy:

1) Ethnicity = Asian/International;
2) CA students have "geographic" advantage
3) Apply to all majors
4) Sports would not help, unless you are "recruited."

Emory University

A) Ethnicity

White	Asian	Race Unknown	Int'l Students
43%	23%	7%	11%

B) Admission Rates

Overall Admit Rate	Regular Admit Rate	Early Action/Early Decision
25.9%	24.7%	49%

C) Test Scores

SAT	**25 Percentile**	**75 Percentile**
Reading	640	740
Math	670	760
Writing	650	750
ACT	30	33

D) Financial Aid

% 1st Yr Student Receiving Grants	Avg Grants 1st Yr Student	Total Cost of Attendance (COA)
45%	$32,425	$55,992

E) Majors and Fields of Study

% Degrees in Math, Sci/Engr	Degrees in Other
20%	80%

Emory University

Emory (along with Duke) is probably the most well-known Southern school among Asian parents and students. Chart A confirms that as it shows a 23% Asian population. Located in Atlanta, Georgia, Emory is ranked 20th by *U.S. News*. It has approx. 7,200 undergrad enrollment (slightly higher than Duke and Vanderbilt). Emory has a gender gap, with 55% female vs. 45% male.

Money Matters & Career

45% of Emory 1st year students receive an average grant of $32,425 (Chart D). Against a COA (Cost of Attendance) of $55,992 that amounts to be a 58% discount off the full price. Emory's 58% discounts is behind Duke (64%), Vanderbilt (66%), and the Ivy League average (63%). However, Emory is ranked behind all these schools, so this 58% discount is reasonable.

For mid-career (15 years experience) salary, Emory grads report an average of $90K, according to www.payscale.com. This $90K amounts falls short vs. schools that are ranked near Emory. Specifically, Notre Dame ($112K), Carnegie Mellon ($108K), UC-Berkeley ($109K), Vanderbilt ($104K) and Rice ($100K) all report higher mid-career salaries.

As for Ph.D. rate, Emory is not ranked in the top 50 schools whose graduates are likely to obtain Ph.D.'s later on. This is according to Nat'l Science Foundation. Perhaps this is not surprising since 80% of Emory student study areas other than math, science or engineering. However, there are plenty of liberal arts schools listed in the top 50 schools for Ph.D. rate. Thus, the fact that Emory is not ranked in the Nat'l Science Foundation ranking is a concern. Thus, we conclude that Emory is not as generous as other schools ranked close by.

Ethnicity & Leverage

Chart A shows Whites outnumber Asians by almost 2-to-1 only (43% vs. 23%), which is much lower than other schools in the South and East. Thus, just based on ethnicity, Asian don't have leverage when applying to Emory. That means to gain admissions, you would need at least 75 percentile in test score. To receive a financial aid offer that is more than the average (Chart D), you would need test scores (as well as great GPA) in the 90 percentile range.

Furthermore, Emory is still draws most of its students (including Asians) from East. Thus, CA applicants would have "geographic diversity" advantage.

Athletics to the Rescue?

Yes. Student-athletes applying to Emory will have an advantage because Emory compete in Div. III (least competitive). However, several of Emory teams are have "elite" status. Specially, Emory's women's swimming team finished as 2011 Div. III Champion this past spring (men's team finished 3rd). Thus, for swimming, applicants cannot just be "average" level. A good rule of thumb is as follows: for male swimmers (under 21 seconds for 50 yards freestyle), and for female (under 24 seconds for 50 yards freestyle). We use swimming as an example because West coast swimmers usually have an advantage due to higher time standards.

You Can Study Science as well as Liberal Arts

Chart E. shows that plenty of student study science/engineering at Emory (20%). Specifically, 14% study Engineering and 5% study Biology. Among non-science majors, Business (17%) is the overwhelming favorite, and with Economics (7.5%) a distant second.

Conclusion

In summary, the following "strategies" will increase your chances at Emory and financial aid:

1) Be male (female = 55% at Emory);
2) Apply Early (where acceptance rate = 44; Chart B);
3) Ethnicity = International
4) CA students have "geographic" advantage;
5) Student-athlete (quick review of Emory sports teams shows very few Asian athletes);
6) Apply to all majors.

Tulane University

A) Ethnicity

White	Asian	Race Unknown	Int'l Students
63%	4%	13%	3%

B) Admission Rates

Overall Admit Rate	Regular Admit Rate	Early Action/Early Decision
26%	NA	NA

C) Test Scores

SAT	25 Percentile	75 Percentile
Reading	610	700
Math	620	700
Writing	630	710
ACT	29	32

D) Financial Aid

% 1st Yr Student Receiving Grants	Avg Grants 1st Yr Student	Total Cost of Attendance (COA)
38%	$23,690	$54,258

E) Majors and Fields of Study

% Degrees in Math, Sci/Engr	Degrees in Other
19%	81%

Tulane University

Ranked 51st by *U.S. News*, Tulane is located in New Orleans, Louisiana. With an undergrad enrollment of approximately 6,200, student can study science, engineering, in addition to liberal arts (Chart E.). Just like many other schools, Tulane has a gender gap (56% female v. 44% male). Probably due to its graduate programs, Tulane is actually known to many Asian parents.

Money Matters & Career

38% of Tulane freshmen students receive an average grant of $23,690 (Chart D). Against a total COA (Cost of Attendance) of $55,992, that amounts to a 44% discount for Tulane. This "discount" is pretty low, as other Southern schools profiled all beat this number. Specifically, Emory (58%), Vanderbilt (66%) and Duke (64%) all towers over Tulane's discount. However, we do have to keep in mind those schools are all ranked in the top 20. Thus, Since Tulane is ranked 30 places lower at 51st, 44% may still be reasonable.

For career, according to www.payscale.com, Tulane graduates can expect an average $92.2K of "mid-career" (15 years experience) salary. This figure is just above Northwestern ($91.9K) and UCLA ($91.6K). As we know, UCLA and Northwestern (NW) are ranked much higher, with NW ranking 12th. Thus, this salary number from Tulane is impressive. Against Southern peer schools, Tulane ($92.2K) still best higher-ranked Emory ($90K), but falls short against Vanderbilt ($104K) and Duke ($117K).

As for Ph.D. rate, Tulane is ranked among the top 50 schools whose graduates obtain science/engineering Ph.D.'s later on, according to the National Science Foundation. Perhaps this is understandable, since Tulane is ranked 51st.

Overall, Tulane's discount is perhaps a little low. If a student can obtain an above-average offer, then Tulane becomes generous, during to the better than expected salary report.

Ethnicity & Leverage

Chart B shows that Tulane's acceptance rate (about 25%) is very competitive. This is the approx. admit rate of UCLA. So would ethnicity help Asian applicants here? Chart A shows Whites outnumber Asians by almost 16-to-1 (63% vs. 4%). Thus, Asian applicants have strong leverage for Tulane.

Thus, Asian applicants probably just need to score in the 50 percentile to get in. For Asian males, that requirement should be even lower, since Tulane has 56% female students. For Asian students scoring in the 75 percentile, you are almost certain to gain admissions AND receive a financial aid offer that is more than the average (Chart D).

Sports Help?

Asians are vastly underrepresented at Tulane that sports is not even necessary to help. We believe ethnicity is enough. If you are very good student-athlete, you may want to consider other schools (i.e. higher ranked) where athletics would be relied upon to help you get in.

You Can Study Science as well as Liberal Arts

As seen clearly in Chart E, 19% Tulane students study science/engineering. Not surprisingly, the most popular majors are Biology (10%), with Computer Science (3%) and Engineering (3%) behind. As for non-science/engineering majors, Business (23%) is the most popular.

Conclusion

In summary, the following "strategies" will increase your chances at Tulane and your financial aid:

1) Ethnicity = Asian/International;
2) CA students have "geographic" advantage;
3) Males have slight more advantage;
4) Apply to all majors;
5) Can be viewed as back-up school, if more than enough financial aid is obtained.

Davidson College

A) Ethnicity

White	Asian	Race Unknown	Int'l Students
72%	5%	6%	4%

B) Admission Rates

Overall Admit Rate	Regular Admit Rate	Early Action/Early Decision
24.2%	NA	NA

C) Test Scores

SAT	**25 Percentile**	**75 Percentile**
Reading	630	720
Math	630	710
Writing	620	720
ACT	28	32

D) Financial Aid

% 1st Yr Student Receiving Grants	Avg Grants 1st Yr Student	Total Cost of Attendance (COA)
42%	$27,125	$52,498

E) Majors and Fields of Study

% Degrees in Math, Sci/Engr	Degrees in Other
16%	84%

Davidson College

Davidson College is most likely "unknown" to many Asian students and parents, Davidson is actually a hidden gem. Ranked No. 9 by *U.S. News* for National Liberal Arts Colleges, it is actually ranked ahead of Claremont McKenna (No. 10) and Wesleyan (Little Three Member; No. 12th). Located in Davidson, North Carolina, it is only 26 miles from Charlotte Int'l Airport. Davidson has an undergrad enrollment of 1,700, about the size of Pomona College.

Money Matters & Career

42% of Davidson freshmen students receive an average grant of $27,125. Against a total COA (Cost of Attendance) of $52,498, that amounts to a 52% discount for Davidson. This discount is comparable to Claremont McKenna (51%), but it still falls short vs. Wesleyan (62%), and Univ. of Richmond (64%). Thus, the "out-the-door" price is approx. $25K ($52K-$27K), still less than full-priced UC Schools. If you like a financial aid package of more than average, please see "leverage" section below.

For career, according to www.payscale.com, Davidson graduates earn an average mid-career (15 years experience) salary of $101K, an impressive number for an "unknown" school. Specifically, Davidson's $101K beats well-known schools such as Columbia ($99.7K), Rice ($100K), U. of Chicago ($100K), and USC ($99.4K). We believe that result put Davidson in the "big leagues."

As for Ph.D. rate, Davidson is not ranked in the top 50 schools whose graduates are likely to obtain Ph.D.'s later on. This is according to Nat'l Science Foundation. We are a little surprised by this since many other small liberal arts schools made the top 50 (i.e. Williams, Amherst, Wesleyan, Reed, Pomona, etc.).

Overall, you need to use leverage to gain acceptance into Davidson and see if that results in a nice financial aid offer.

Ethnicity & Leverage

Just like many other liberal arts schools, Asian has leverage when applying to Davidson. Asians are only at 5% in Davidson (vs. 72% White). Furthermore, CA Asian applicants would enjoy even more advantage, due to geographic diversity. Due to leverage, an Asian applicant would need to score in the 50 percentile to get in (even below 50 percentile would have an great chance). Furthermore, if your test scores are at 75 percentile (Chart C), you are like to gain admission with *above average* financial aid offer.

Moreover, the ethnicity factor is big enough that sports do not even need to come into play.

You Can Study Science as well as Liberal Arts

As seen clearly in Chart E, 16% Davidson student math science. Specifically, 9% study Biology, and the rest study Math and Physics. As for non-math/science majors, English (14%) and Political Science (13%) lead the way.

Conclusion

In summary, the following "secrets" will increase your chances significantly at Davidson for admissions and more financial aid:

1) Asian students are "underrepresented" at Davidson (only 5%);
2) Apply to all majors;
3) Apply to all majors. CA students have "geographic" advantage;
4) No need to apply Early Decision because Asians have leverage.

University of Richmond

A) Ethnicity

White	Asian	Race Unknown	Int'l Students
61%	5%	12%	9%

B) Admission Rates

Overall Admit Rate	Regular Admit Rate	Early Action/Early Decision
30%	NA	NA

C) Test Scores

SAT	**25 Percentile**	**75 Percentile**
Reading	580	680
Math	600	700
Writing	600	690
ACT	27	31

D) Financial Aid

% 1st Yr Student Receiving Grants	Avg Grants 1st Yr Student	Total Cost of Attendance (COA)
47%	$33,515	$52,520

E) Majors and Fields of Study

% Degrees in Math, Sci/Engr	Degrees in Other
11%	89%

University of Richmond

Located in capital of Virginia, University of Richmond ('Richmond")'s undergrad enrollment is only 3,000. Two hours from Washington, DC, and 1 hour from Univ. of Virginia, Richmond is ranked 32nd in "Best National Liberal Arts Colleges" by *U.S. News.* There is a gender gap with 54% females vs. 46% male.

Money Matters & Career

47% of Richmond 1st year students receive an average grant of $33,515 (Chart D). Against a COA (Cost of Attendance) of $55,520, that amounts to be a 64% discount off the full price. This discounts compares well with Duke (64%), Vanderbilt (66%), Emory (58%) and the Ivy League average of 63%. Thus, the "out-the-door" price is just $22K ($55.5K-$33.5K), well under full-priced UC schools. Furthermore, Richmond's s discount is also higher than Univ. of Chicago (48%), Northwestern (48%), Carnegie Mellon (43%), and Washington U-St. Louis (41%), all famous schools.

For mid-career (15 years experience) salary, Richmond grads average $86.3K, according to www.payscale.com. This number is quite low, as compared to peer Southern schools. Specifically, Richmond's salary figure is lower than Emory ($90K), Vanderbilt ($104K), Tulane ($92.2K) and Duke ($117K).

As for Ph.D. rate, Richmond is not ranked in the top 50 schools whose graduates are likely to obtain Ph.D.'s later on. This is according to Nat'l Science Foundation. Overall, since Richmond is offering such a high discount, we conclude Richmond is generous. Using leverage, you can perhaps even obtain a better-than-average financial aid award.

Ethnicity & Leverage

Chart A shows Whites outnumber Asians by the ratio of 12-to-1 (61% vs. 5%). Thus, we can conclude Richmond would seek to recruit excellent Asian students, and thus Asians would have leverage.

With that in mind, then Asian students would probably need to be at least the 25 percentile test scores to gain acceptance (Chart C). If you like an *above average* financial aid offer, then you need to have test scores around 50 percentile.

As mentioned, the best approach for Richmond is to make it a top back-up school. You should apply to UC schools, MIT, Johns Hopkins, etc. as well as "generous" back-up schools like Richmond. If you fail to gain admission to those more famous schools, and if Richmond give you a nice financial aid package, then you should seriously consider it.

You Can Study Science as well as Liberal Arts

Chart E. shows that plenty of student study science/engineering at Richmond (11%). Specifically, 6% study Biology and the rest study Math and Physics. Among non-science majors, Business (35%) is the overwhelming favorite.

Conclusion

In summary, the following "strategies" will increase your chances at Richmond:

1) Be female (female = 54% at Richmond);
2) Ethnicity = Asian/International
3) CA students have "geographic" advantage;
4) Apply to all majors;
5) No need to apply Early Decision because of leverage.

PART III: Let the Games Begin

PART III: Let the Games Begin

Since this book is sports-themed, we thought it would be interesting to allow schools compete against each other, in the "field" of financial aid. Each year at the annual NCAA basketball tournament (commonly known as "March Madness") small schools compete against larger schools. To the surprise of many, smaller schools matched up very well against larger schools. In fact, several small schools have "upset" well-known schools by defeating them.

By the same token, many high school students also have their own "March Madness" in late March/early April of each year. By that time, they have received acceptances and financial aid offers from several schools. They would need to decide what is the best school, in terms of academics and financial aid.

Thus, we want to see whether smaller or lesser-known schools can compete with highly ranked (and more famous) schools in financial aid and career. Will there be any "upsets"? Here are the games. Let the games begin.

Columbia vs.	Haverford
USC vs.	NYU
Wellesley vs.	UCLA
Northwestern vs.	UC-Berkeley
UC-Irvine vs.	Reed
Cornell vs.	Johns Hopkins
Rice vs.	Washington Univ. – St. Louis
Schools That Are "Over-rated" vs.	Schools That Are "Under-rated"

Columbia University vs. Haverford College

Since this book is about comparisons, then let's look at Columbia vs. Haverford. If we take a survey of 100 Asian parents and students from CA and ask them which of these 2 schools they like to attend, 99 (possibly 100) would say Columbia. Half of them may never heard of Haverford. Here is a quick summary of both schools:

	Columbia	**Haverford**
Admit Rate	7.4% ("Almost Impossible to get In")	25% ("Reasonable")
U.S. News Ranking	4th for Nat'l Univ.	9th for Liberal Arts
% 1st Students Receive Need-Based Grants	47%	47%
Avg. Grants/1st Yr.	$32,915	$34,673
Mid-Career Salary	$99,700	$102,000
Science/Engr. Ph.D. rate	Not ranked in the top 50	Ranked 13th (9.5%)
Student-faculty ratio	6-to-1	8-to-1

Just like the NCAA basketball tournament, small schools can give "trouble" to big schools. Here, it may appear at first that Columbia is the clear choice. But Haverford performs great in the category of (1) mid-career salary, and (2) science/engr. Ph.D. rate. For salary, the numbers are actually very close. Many would think Columbia would win the salary category by a mile. Did not happen.

Furthermore, most people probably cannot believe that a "liberal arts" like Haverford can have a higher percentage of graduates in Ph.D. than world-famous Columbia. And it is not even close as Haverford is ranked 13th in this category, and Columbia is not ranked in the top-50.

We are <u>not</u> suggesting you don't applying to Columbia or similar high-ranking schools. We are suggesting you apply to <u>both</u> Columbia AND Haverford. Since the <u>failure</u> rate for Columbia admissions is almost 94%, then there is a good chance you get rejected from Columbia but receive admission to Haverford. In that case, Haverford would be an excellent choice. Just as the proverb states: "We should not judge a book by its cover", the fact that we have not heard of a college does not mean it's a bad school. In summary, that are many "good" schools out there. Asian parents and students need to expand the definition of "good" schools.

USC v. NYU

How about a "heavyweight" battle between East and West Coast? These 2 schools have done an excellent job of marketing in recent years, projecting themselves as the "cool" school of either coast. Sunshine/Hollywood LA vs. trendy/cosmopolitan NYC. Who is going to win this battle? If this is in sports, then USC would dominate for sure. But this is academics and financial aid. According to U.S. News, they are close in ranking: USC (23rd) vs. NYC (33rd).

	USC	**NYU**
Admit Rate	18%	33%
U.S. News Ranking	23rd	33rd
% 1st Students Receive Need-Based Grants	63%	51%
Avg. Grant/1st Yr	$26,112	$19,120
"Discount"= Avg. Grants/Total Cost	45%	34%
% Students Study Business	26%	14%
Mid-Career Salary	$99,400	$88,800
Science/Engr. Ph.D. rate	Not ranked in top-50	Not ranked in top-50
Student-faculty ratio	9-to-1	11-to-1

Frankly, we are a little mystified on how NYU can be ranked so high (33rd). USC wins all categories hands-down. Specifically, USC provides more of a discount for its costs and a higher dollar amount for average grants. Even for those NYU students who do receive grants, it is a paltry $19K only (not even enough money for one semester).

And in the very important mid-career salary category, NYU comes up short (way short) vs. USC. This is very surprising since salaries in New York are "supposed" to be higher. Based on these factors, we believe USC holds up its ranking well and wins this battle decisively.

Furthermore, due to the fact that NYU is "not-so-generous", we suggest you apply to other schools that provide more financial aid.

UCLA vs. Wellesley

We have good cross-country duel here. Let's say you are a female student and you are deciding Wellesley vs. UCLA? Which school would come out on top?

	UCLA	**Wellesley**
Admit Rate	21.3%	31% (all-female)
U.S. News Ranking	25th - Nat'l Universities	4th – Nat'l Liberal Arts schools
% 1st Students Receive Need-Based Grants	47%	61%
Avg. Grant/1st Yr	$13,643	$36,508
"Discount"= Avg. Grants/Total Cost	45%	69%
Mid-Career Salary	$91,600	$84,600
Science/Engr. Ph.D. rate	Not ranked in top-50	33rd (6.5%)
Student-faculty ratio	17-to-1	8-to-1

Clearly, UCLA holds the upper hand in admit rate. Among CA residents, UCLA may hold a higher reputation. But Wellesley is highly respected around the U.S. With a strong alumni network, Wellesley is able to provide very generous financial aid, with a 69% discount to qualified (61% of 1st Yr) students. Despite its reputation as a "liberal arts school", Wellesley is ranked 33rd in science/engr. Ph.D. rate, while UCLA is not ranked in the top-50.

UCLA does beat Wellesley in mid-career salary. However, as we explained in the Wellesley section, that is probably due to the fact that many of its alumni is working for the government, where salary is lower. But we also analyzed that the influence of such alumni is much stronger than salary numbers. We believe Wellesley should "win" this match-up.

Again, we would suggest the student to apply to both schools. And if you can get into UCLA and Wellesley, you should take the above factors – not just rankings – into consideration. If you do not gain admission to UCLA but does get into Wellesley (a very likely scenario since UCLA has lower admit rate), then you should rejoice.

UC-Berkeley vs. Northwestern

This is a dilemma that many CA students confront each year: UC-Berkeley (top CA public school) or a high-ranking out-of-state private school such as Northwestern (ranked 12th). With all the budget cutbacks and tuition increases in the UC system, is it still worth it to attend the "top UC" rather than a top private school like NW? Let's see how they compare:

	UC-Berkeley	**Northwestern**
Admit Rate	21.1%	15.3%
U.S. News Ranking	22nd	12th
% 1st Students Receive Need-Based Grants	46%	46%
Avg. Grant/1st Yr	$17,468	$27,968
"Discount"= Avg. Grants/Total Cost	55%	48%
Mid-Career Salary	$109,000	$91,900
Science/Engr. Ph.D. rate	39th (5.7%)	Not ranked in top-50
Student-faculty ratio	17-to-1	7-to-1

As expected, it would be not an easy decision, with both schools evenly matched in many categories above. NW has a lower admit rate and a much lower student-to-faculty ratio. However, UC-Berkeley provides more of a discount (55% vs. 48%).

However, the deciding factor for us is the mid-career salary. NW somehow cannot keep up with UC-Berkeley in mid-career salary, losing by $17K (19% difference). Furthermore, Berkeley students are ranked 39th in the U.S. in the likelihood of obtaining science/engr. Ph.D.'s. NW is not ranked in the top-50 schools.

Thus, we believe UC-Berkeley wins this battle easily. As we discussed in the Berkeley section, we believe it should be ranked much higher in *U.S. News* rankings. One must really wonder how a school is ranked 12th (Northwestern), but performs so poorly in mid-career salary category. Just base on that alone, UC-Berkeley should be ranked *ahead* of Northwestern.

UC-Irvine vs. Reed College

This looks another "mis-match" as UC-Irvine is ranked 41st In U.S. News, and received more 44,000 applications in 2010. So on one hand, it is a popular school (UC-Irvine) vs. an virtual unknown. Despite being on the West Coast (Portland), many people probably have heard of Reed (1,400 undergrads). Let's see how they compare:

	UC-Irvine	Reed (Portland, Ore.)
Admit Rate	36.3%	34.1%
U.S. News Ranking	41st	54th (Liberal Arts)
% 1st Students Receive Need-Based Grants	50%	46%
Avg. Grant/1st Yr	$12,406	$34,939
"Discount"= Avg. Grants/Total Cost	44%	63%
Mid-Career Salary	$92,500	$86,100
Science/Engr. Ph.D. rate	Not ranked in top-50	4th (13.8%)
Student-faculty ratio	19-to-1	10-to-1

These 2 schools' admit rate is practically the same, and UC-Irvine has a higher mid-career salary. However, Reed is no push-over. Reed provides much more financial aid, in terms of dollar amount and percentage discount. And it is the 4th ranked school in the U.S. on terms of science/engr. Ph.D. rates (behind only Cal Tech, Harvey Mudd and MIT). Furthermore, there is no comparison in the category of student-to-faculty ratio as Reed wins hands down.

Thus, we are saying again private schools (when taking into account financial aid), is perhaps a better deal than UC schools.

Therefore, we are suggesting you apply to <u>both</u> UC-Irvine and Reed. If you get admitted to both, then you can compare financial aid offers from both schools. Based on the "out-the-door" price, then you can decide which school is cost-effective. If the "out-the-door" price is similar, you should consider picking Reed because of its education would have solid "return" (Ph. D. rate).

Cornell vs. Johns Hopkins

How about a match of two top-15 schools known for science/engineering and liberal arts? These two schools are not just rivals academically, but also fierce "enemies" in men's lacrosse. The rivalry dates back to 1977, when Cornell beat Hopkins to win NCAA Championship. Ten years later in 1987, Hopkins returned the favor by beating Cornell in the Finals. Here, according *to U.S. News'* rankings, they are close as well: Cornell (15th) vs. Johns Hopkins (13th).

	Cornell	**Johns Hopkins**
Admit Rate	16.2%	17.7%
U.S. News Ranking	15th	13th
% 1st Students Receive Need-Based Grants	51%	51%
Avg. Grant/1st Yr	$33,653	$30,791
"Discount"= Avg. Grants/Total Cost	59%	53%
Science/Engr. Ph.D. rate	22nd (7.6%)	20th (7.7%)
Mid-Career Salary	$106,000	$90,100
% Students majoring in Math, Science/Engr.	42%	60%
Student-faculty ratio	9-to-1	11-to-1

Wow, everything about these Cornell and JHU schools is just as expected: they are very close in each category. In its favor, Cornell has a slightly lower admit rate and higher discount for financial aid. Johns Hopkins has a slightly higher Ph.D. rate for science/engineering. The student-to-faculty ratio is practically the same.

For mid-career salary, one would expect that since Hopkins has more science/engineering students (60% vs. 42%), it should have to have a much higher salary than Cornell. But it turns out that Cornell's salary has a huge discrepancy over Hopkins (a 18% advantage over Hopkins).

As explained in the Johns Hopkins section, it is a little surprising to see a school like Hopkins' caliber to score under $100K in mid-career salary. Cornell, like other science & engineering schools, score as expected in the salary category. Thus, we believe Cornell should get the "win" here based largely on the salary category.

Thus, for science/engineering students, you should apply to both. If you get admitted to both, you can use the above analysis. If you only gain admissions to either Cornell or Hopkins, then you would receive an excellent education at either school.

Rice University vs. Washington Univ.-St. Louis

Like the NCAA basketball tournament, it's time to compete against each other. Let's take a look at two closely ranked schools in the Midwest: Rice vs. Washington Univ.-St. Louis ("WUSTL"). Of the two schools, WUSTL is the more famous among Asian students and parents.

	Rice	**WUSTL**
Admit Rate	18%	17.9%
U.S. News Ranking	17th	13th
% 1st Students Receive Need-Based Grants	68%	57%
Avg. Grant/1st Yr	$25,851	$23,513
"Discount"= Avg. Grants/Total Cost	53%	41%
Mid-Career Salary	$100,000	$91,400
Science/Engr. Ph.D. rate	9th (10.5%)	Not ranked in top-50
Student-faculty ratio	6-to-1	7-to-1

Looks like we have another "upset" here. The lowered-ranked Rice beats WUSTL in almost every category above. While the admit rate is the same for both, financial aid favors Rice heavily as it is the more "generous" school. After the graduations, Rice wins the "mid-career" salary hands down. As for Ph.D. rate, there is no comparison as Rice is ranked 9th in the entire U.S., while WUSTL is ranked outside of the top-50. In summary, Rice should probably move up in the U.S. News rankings and WUSTL should slide down. Thus, Rice is clearly the decisive victor here.

In our East Coast example (Columbia vs. Haverford), we suggested applying to both schools. Here, we suggest just apply to Rice and not WUSTL, because Rice is the clear choice here.

Overrated vs. Underrated Schools

If you going to pay almost ***$240K*** for college (private school full price), presumably you want to receive some financial aid, and see if such high tuition translate into a good salary later one. Based on our research and the above "battles," here is a list of overrated and underrated generous schools with respect to financial aid:

Most Overrated	**Most Underrated**
Northwestern	Brown
Johns Hopkins	Cornell
Washington Univ. – St. Louis (WUSTL)	Rice

Financial Aid & Mid-Career Salary Falls Short

Northwestern (12th), Johns Hopkins (13th) and WUSTL (13th) are ranked highly by *U.S. News*. However, when it comes to financial aid, they are not generous as compared to similar ranked schools (please see each school's specific section for detailed numbers). In fact, their financial aid package fall well short against the under-rated schools listed above.

As for mid-career (15 years experience) salary, NW, Johns Hopkins and WUSTL all average around $90K. Surely when you attend a top-15th school, you expect salary to be higher. For example, how is it possible for a school like Johns Hopkins, where science and engineering are their specialty, to have a salary figure ($90K) close to "artsy" NYU? In fact, these 3 overrated schools are the *only ones* ranked in the top-20 by *U.S. News* that have salary hovering around $90K (the other 17 schools are all $100K or above). This statistic itself is enough to justify our assertion that these schools are overrated.

In addition to good salary numbers, Brown, Cornell and Rice all placed in the top-50 schools in terms of Ph.D. rate for its undergraduates. At the very least, the Ph.D. rate measure intellectual capacity of the student body. Only Johns Hopkins made the top-50, while NW and WUSTL did not. Thus, we can reasonably conclude that the caliber of students in Rice, Cornell and Brown all beat the 3 overrated schools.

Underrated Schools' Strengths

Ranked only 15th by *U. S. News*, Brown is possibly the *most* underrated schools here. By attracting all all-time high in applications for incoming Class of 2015, Brown had an all-time low acceptance rate of *8.7%* (better than all 3 overrated schools). By allowing students to design their own majors and course of study, Brown students thrive because the world changes faster than the traditional curriculum. As for money, 49% of Brown 1st year students receives a huge 64% discount off the sticker price. Brown should vault ahead of the 3 overrated schools into the *top-10*, where it belongs.

Despite the fact that it is named an university, Rice only has about 3,200 undergrads, just a little larger than many American high schools. This smaller environment just encourage learning and bonding among students. 68% of Rice 1st year student received over $25K in grants underscore its generosity. Rice should be a couple notches below Brown but above the 3 overrated schools.

Cornell's strengths lie in the availability of majors and courses. The wide spectrum, from math/science/engineering, traditional liberal arts, to esoteric majors such as animal science, is perhaps the widest of any school in America. Money? 51% of Cornell 1st year students receive over 59% off the sticker price. Cornell should be tied with Rice and above the 3 overrated schools.

EPILOGUE

EPILOGUE

We hope this book would open our readers mind in looking at college admissions and financial aid. They are actually *integrated* since you must get in to receive financial aid. We wrote this book to open eyes and mind, because we feel the information out in the Asian community is not to propel students into the elite schools. In this book, you have found we outlined a detailed strategy for each elite school profiled in the book.

Discrimination?

With admission rates in top schools dropping like the weight of gravity, some Asian parents and students are clearly disappointed and wonder how top schools can be "conquered." In the mass-circulation Chinese World Journal, there was even a recent article (1) stating it's almost impossible for Asian to get into top schools, and (2) alleging discrimination against Asian student by top schools.

We absolutely disagree with the above 2 statements. In this book, we have outlined in detail the strategies for admission into the top schools. Furthermore, based on our research for this book, we disagree with the notion that discrimination exists against Asian students. We believe the primary reason Asian students gets rejected is because they don't know the "rules." As Sun-Tzu stated 2,500 years ago, "if you do not know yourself and your opponent, you will lose in battle every time" against your opponent. The "opponents" in the college game are Harvard, Yale, Princeton, etc. We are writing this book to tell the Asian community what the rules are.

Thus, before anyone alleges discrimination, we need to ask: have the typical Asian applicant engage in activities outlined in this book? For example, if someone can show us an example of an Asian football quarterback getting rejected from the Ivy League despite good grades, then we would agree it is discrimination. But there are so few – if any – quarterbacks in the Ivy League that they would welcome that candidate with open arms. Similarly, if an Asian student-athlete who has participated in "cool" activities like lifeguard, but have been getting rejected from the Ivy League despite meeting athletic and academic standards, then it looks like discrimination.

No Complaining & I-CAN Attitude

Therefore, Asian students should participate in sports and Lifeguard to show coolness and stand out. We find it encouraging that many Asian applicants try their best to present an academic image of "fit" to the top schools, such as top grades, SAT scores, tough curriculum, etc. So the missing piece for most Asians students is the "personality" image projection.

Throughout this book, we have offered numerous solutions as well as strategies for each particular school. This book is based on the ideas of *Art of War* by Sun-Tzu and judo, concepts that originate from Asia. If Asian students are to win the "College & Financial Aid Game," then we must follow the concepts in the *Art of War* and judo. We must use our strengths and use that against the opponents' weakness. Each school's weakness is outlined here in this book.

Instead of complaining, we can follow learn an important concept from the *Art of War*. "If you know yourself and your opponent, you will be victorious in every battle against your opponent." Moreover, we need to remember this is America, and the last 4 letters of the word "American" is "I CAN." With an indomitable American spirit and Asian concepts *Art of War* and judo, Asian students can win the American College and Financial Aid Game.

Bibliography

Part I

General References	Sun Tzu, *Art of War* (translated Ralph D. Sawyer), Westview Press Inc. (1994)
	U. S. News & World Report , Best Colleges, 2011 Edition
	Joan Burrelli, Allan Rapoport and Rolf Lehming, *Baccalaureate Origin of S & E Doctorate Recipients*, National Science Foundation, Directorate for Social, Behavioral, and Economic Sciences (July 2008)
	www.payscale.com; http://www.payscale.com/2010-best-colleges/top-us-colleges-graduate-salary-statistics.asp
	Allen M. Leung, *Legal Judo: Strategic Applications of Reexamination Versus an Aggressive Adversary (Part I)*, 84 J. Pat. & Trademark Off. Soc'y 471 (June 2002)
	Allen M. Leung, *Legal Judo: Strategic Applications of Reexamination Versus an Aggressive Adversary (Part II)*, 84 J. Pat. & Trademark Off. Soc'y 553 (July 2002)

Part II

Conference One: Ivy League	**Source**
Harvard	Common Data Set available at www.harvard.edu; U.S. Dept of Education, Institute of Educational Sciences, Nat'l Center for Education Statistics (http://nces.ed.gov/collegenavigator/); *The Crimson*, March 31, 2011, http://www.thecrimson.com/article/2011/3/31/percent-class-students-year/
Yale	Common Data Set available at www.yale.edu; U.S. Dept of Education, Institute of Educational Sciences, Nat'l Center for Education Statistics (http://nces.ed.gov/collegenavigator/); *Yale Daily News*, March 31, 2011 http://www.yaledailynews.com/news/2011/mar/31/class-admit-rate-lower-rate/
Princeton	Common Data Set available at www.princeton.edu; U.S. Dept of Education, Institute of Educational Sciences, Nat'l Center for Education Statistics (http://nces.ed.gov/collegenavigator/); www.princeton.edu/main/news/archive/S30/15/00I77/index.xml?section=topstories
Brown	Common Data Set available at www.brown.edu; U.S. Dept of Education, Institute of Educational Sciences, Nat'l Center for Education Statistics (http://nces.ed.gov/collegenavigator/); The *Brown Daily Herald*, April 4, 2011, http://www.browndailyherald.com/university-admits-record-low-8-7-percent-of-applicants-1.2530595
Columbia	Common Data Set available at www.columbia.edu; U.S. Dept of Education, Institute of Educational Sciences, Nat'l Center for Education Statistics (http://nces.ed.gov/collegenavigator/); *The Columbia Spectator*, March 30, 2011, http://www.columbiaspectator.com/2011/03/30/cc-admit-rate-drops-64-percent

Cornell	Common Data Set available at www.cornell.edu; U.S. Dept of Education, Institute of Educational Sciences, Nat'l Center for Education Statistics (http://nces.ed.gov/collegenavigator/); *The Cornell Sun*, March 31, 2011, http://cornellsun.com/section/news/content/2011/03/31/admissions-rate-drops-class-2015
Dartmouth	Common Data Set available at www.dartmouth.edu; U.S. Dept of Education, Institute of Educational Sciences, Nat'l Center for Education Statistics (http://nces.ed.gov/collegenavigator/); *The Dartmouth,* March 31, 2011, http://thedartmouth.com/2011/03/31/news/admission
UPenn	Common Data Set available at www.upenn.edu; U.S. Dept of Education, Institute of Educational Sciences, Nat'l Center for Education Statistics (http://nces.ed.gov/collegenavigator/); *The Daily Pennsylvanian*, March 31, 2011, http://www.dailypennsylvanian.com/article/admissions-rate-drops-123-percent
Conference Two: Little Ivies/NESCAC	
Williams	Common Data Set available at www.williams.edu; U.S. Dept of Education, Institute of Educational Sciences, Nat'l Center for Education Statistics (http://nces.ed.gov/collegenavigator/)
Amherst	Common Data Set available at www.amherst.edu; U.S. Dept of Education, Institute of Educational Sciences, Nat'l Center for Education Statistics (http://nces.ed.gov/collegenavigator/)
Wesleyan	Common Data Set available at www.wesleyan.edu; U.S. Dept of Education, Institute of Educational Sciences, Nat'l Center for Education Statistics (http://nces.ed.gov/collegenavigator/)
Bates	Common Data Set available at www.bates.edu; U.S. Dept of Education, Institute of Educational Sciences, Nat'l Center for Education Statistics (http://nces.ed.gov/collegenavigator/)
Bowdoin	Common Data Set available at www.bowdoin.edu; U.S. Dept of Education, Institute of Educational Sciences, Nat'l Center for Education Statistics (http://nces.ed.gov/collegenavigator/)
Colby	Common Data Set available at www.colby.edu; U.S. Dept of Education, Institute of Educational Sciences, Nat'l Center for Education Statistics (http://nces.ed.gov/collegenavigator/)
Middlebury	Common Data Set available at www.middlebury.edu; U.S. Dept of Education, Institute of Educational Sciences, Nat'l Center for Education Statistics (http://nces.ed.gov/collegenavigator/)
Haverford	Common Data Set available at www.haverford.edu; U.S. Dept of Education, Institute of Educational Sciences, Nat'l Center for Education Statistics (http://nces.ed.gov/collegenavigator/)
Swarthmore	Common Data Set available at www.swarthmore.edu;

	U.S. Dept of Education, Institute of Educational Sciences, Nat'l Center for Education Statistics (http://nces.ed.gov/collegenavigator/)
Conference Three: West Coast Elite	
Stanford	Common Data Set available at www.stanford.edu; U.S. Dept of Education, Institute of Educational Sciences, Nat'l Center for Education Statistics (http://nces.ed.gov/collegenavigator/); *The Stanford Daily*, March 29, 2011, http://www.stanforddaily.com/2011/03/29/stanford-accepts-2427-high-school-applicants/
USC	Common Data Set available at www.usc.edu; U.S. Dept of Education, Institute of Educational Sciences, Nat'l Center for Education Statistics (http://nces.ed.gov/collegenavigator/)
Cal Tech	Common Data Set available at www.caltech.edu; U.S. Dept of Education, Institute of Educational Sciences, Nat'l Center for Education Statistics (http://nces.ed.gov/collegenavigator/)
Harvey Mudd	Common Data Set available at www.hmc.edu; U.S. Dept of Education, Institute of Educational Sciences, Nat'l Center for Education Statistics (http://nces.ed.gov/collegenavigator/)
Pomona	Common Data Set available at www.pomona.edu; U.S. Dept of Education, Institute of Educational Sciences, Nat'l Center for Education Statistics (http://nces.ed.gov/collegenavigator/)
Claremont McKenna	Common Data Set available at www.cmc.edu; U.S. Dept of Education, Institute of Educational Sciences, Nat'l Center for Education Statistics (http://nces.ed.gov/collegenavigator/)
Scripps	Common Data Set available at www.scrippscollege.edu; U.S. Dept of Education, Institute of Educational Sciences, Nat'l Center for Education Statistics (http://nces.ed.gov/collegenavigator/)
Reed	Common Data Set available at www.reed.edu; U.S. Dept of Education, Institute of Educational Sciences, Nat'l Center for Education Statistics (http://nces.ed.gov/collegenavigator/)
Santa Clara	Common Data Set available at www.scu.edu; U.S. Dept of Education, Institute of Educational Sciences, Nat'l Center for Education Statistics (http://nces.ed.gov/collegenavigator/)
Univ. of Pacific	Common Data Set available at web.pacific.edu; U.S. Dept of Education, Institute of Educational Sciences, Nat'l Center for Education Statistics (http://nces.ed.gov/collegenavigator/)
Conference Four: East Coast Elite (Small to Mid-Szie)	
Wellesley	Common Data Set available at www.wellesley.edu; U.S. Dept of Education, Institute of Educational Sciences, Nat'l Center for Education

	Statistics (http://nces.ed.gov/collegenavigator/)
Barnard	Common Data Set available at www.barnard.edu; U.S. Dept of Education, Institute of Educational Sciences, Nat'l Center for Education Statistics (http://nces.ed.gov/collegenavigator/)
Bryn Mawr	Common Data Set available at www.brynmawr.edu; U.S. Dept of Education, Institute of Educational Sciences, Nat'l Center for Education Statistics (http://nces.ed.gov/collegenavigator/)
Vassar	Common Data Set available at www.vassar.edu; U.S. Dept of Education, Institute of Educational Sciences, Nat'l Center for Education Statistics (http://nces.ed.gov/collegenavigator/)
Brandeis	Common Data Set available at www.brandeis.edu; U.S. Dept of Education, Institute of Educational Sciences, Nat'l Center for Education Statistics (http://nces.ed.gov/collegenavigator/)
Olin	Common Data Set available at www.olin.edu; U.S. Dept of Education, Institute of Educational Sciences, Nat'l Center for Education Statistics (http://nces.ed.gov/collegenavigator/)
Colgate	Common Data Set available at www.colgate.edu; U.S. Dept of Education, Institute of Educational Sciences, Nat'l Center for Education Statistics (http://nces.ed.gov/collegenavigator/)
Bucknell	Common Data Set available at www.bucknell.edu; U.S. Dept of Education, Institute of Educational Sciences, Nat'l Center for Education Statistics (http://nces.ed.gov/collegenavigator/)
Lehigh	Common Data Set available at www.lehigh.edu; U.S. Dept of Education, Institute of Educational Sciences, Nat'l Center for Education Statistics (http://nces.ed.gov/collegenavigator/)
Conference Five: East Coast **Elite (Mid to Large)**	
MIT	Common Data Set available at web.mit.edu; U.S. Dept of Education, Institute of Educational Sciences, Nat'l Center for Education Statistics (http://nces.ed.gov/collegenavigator/)
Boston College	Common Data Set available at www.bc.edu; U.S. Dept of Education, Institute of Educational Sciences, Nat'l Center for Education Statistics (http://nces.ed.gov/collegenavigator/)
Boston University	Common Data Set available at www.bu.edu; U.S. Dept of Education, Institute of Educational Sciences, Nat'l Center for Education Statistics (http://nces.ed.gov/collegenavigator/)
Tufts	Common Data Set available at www.tufts.edu; U.S. Dept of Education, Institute of Educational Sciences, Nat'l Center for Education Statistics (http://nces.ed.gov/collegenavigator/)
Georgetown	Common Data Set available at www.georgetown.edu; U.S. Dept of Education, Institute of Educational Sciences, Nat'l Center for Education

	Statistics (http://nces.ed.gov/collegenavigator/)
George Washington	Common Data Set available at www.gwu.edu; U.S. Dept of Education, Institute of Educational Sciences, Nat'l Center for Education Statistics (http://nces.ed.gov/collegenavigator/)
Johns Hopkins	Common Data Set available at www.jhu.edu; U.S. Dept of Education, Institute of Educational Sciences, Nat'l Center for Education Statistics (http://nces.ed.gov/collegenavigator/)
NYU	Common Data Set available at www.nyu.edu; U.S. Dept of Education, Institute of Educational Sciences, Nat'l Center for Education Statistics (http://nces.ed.gov/collegenavigator/)
RPI	Common Data Set available at www.rpi.edu; U.S. Dept of Education, Institute of Educational Sciences, Nat'l Center for Education Statistics (http://nces.ed.gov/collegenavigator/)
Conference Six: Midwest Elite	
Univ. of Chicago	Common Data Set available at www.uchicago.edu; U.S. Dept of Education, Institute of Educational Sciences, Nat'l Center for Education Statistics (http://nces.ed.gov/collegenavigator/)
Northwestern	Common Data Set available at www.northwestern.edu; U.S. Dept of Education, Institute of Educational Sciences, Nat'l Center for Education Statistics (http://nces.ed.gov/collegenavigator/)
Rice	Common Data Set available at www.rice.edu; U.S. Dept of Education, Institute of Educational Sciences, Nat'l Center for Education Statistics (http://nces.ed.gov/collegenavigator/)
Washington Univ. – St. Louis	Common Data Set available at www.wustl.edu; U.S. Dept of Education, Institute of Educational Sciences, Nat'l Center for Education Statistics (http://nces.ed.gov/collegenavigator/)
Notre Dame	Common Data Set available at www.nd.edu; U.S. Dept of Education, Institute of Educational Sciences, Nat'l Center for Education Statistics (http://nces.ed.gov/collegenavigator/)
Oberlin	Common Data Set available at www.oberlin.edu; U.S. Dept of Education, Institute of Educational Sciences, Nat'l Center for Education Statistics (http://nces.ed.gov/collegenavigator/)
Carleton	Common Data Set available at www.carleton.edu; U.S. Dept of Education, Institute of Educational Sciences, Nat'l Center for Education Statistics (http://nces.ed.gov/collegenavigator/)
Macalester	Common Data Set available at www.macalester.edu; U.S. Dept of Education, Institute of Educational Sciences, Nat'l Center for Education Statistics (http://nces.ed.gov/collegenavigator/)
Carnegie Mellon	Common Data Set available at www.cmu.edu; U.S. Dept of Education, Institute of Educational Sciences, Nat'l Center for Education

	Statistics (http://nces.ed.gov/collegenavigator/)
Case Western	Common Data Set available at www.case.edu; U.S. Dept of Education, Institute of Educational Sciences, Nat'l Center for Education Statistics (http://nces.ed.gov/collegenavigator/)
Conference Seven: Select UC Schools	
UC-Berkeley	Common Data Set available at www.berkeley.edu; U.S. Dept of Education, Institute of Educational Sciences, Nat'l Center for Education Statistics (http://nces.ed.gov/collegenavigator/)
UCLA	Common Data Set available at www.ucla.edu; U.S. Dept of Education, Institute of Educational Sciences, Nat'l Center for Education Statistics (http://nces.ed.gov/collegenavigator/)
UC-San Diego	Common Data Set available at www.ucsd.edu; U.S. Dept of Education, Institute of Educational Sciences, Nat'l Center for Education Statistics (http://nces.ed.gov/collegenavigator/)
UC-Irvine	Common Data Set available at www.uci.edu; U.S. Dept of Education, Institute of Educational Sciences, Nat'l Center for Education Statistics (http://nces.ed.gov/collegenavigator/)
UC-Davis	Common Data Set available at www.ucdavis.edu; U.S. Dept of Education, Institute of Educational Sciences, Nat'l Center for Education Statistics (http://nces.ed.gov/collegenavigator/)
UC-Santa Barbara	Common Data Set available at www.ucsb.edu; U.S. Dept of Education, Institute of Educational Sciences, Nat'l Center for Education Statistics (http://nces.ed.gov/collegenavigator/)
Cal Poly-SLO	Common Data Set available at www.calpoly.edu; U.S. Dept of Education, Institute of Educational Sciences, Nat'l Center for Education Statistics (http://nces.ed.gov/collegenavigator/)
Conference Eight: South Elite	
Duke	Common Data Set available at www.duke.edu; U.S. Dept of Education, Institute of Educational Sciences, Nat'l Center for Education Statistics (http://nces.ed.gov/collegenavigator/)
Vanderbilt	Common Data Set available at www.vanderbilt.edu; U.S. Dept of Education, Institute of Educational Sciences, Nat'l Center for Education Statistics (http://nces.ed.gov/collegenavigator/)
Emory	Common Data Set available at www.emory.edu; U.S. Dept of Education, Institute of Educational Sciences, Nat'l Center for Education Statistics (http://nces.ed.gov/collegenavigator/)
Tulane	Common Data Set available at www.tulane.edu;

	U.S. Dept of Education, Institute of Educational Sciences, Nat'l Center for Education Statistics (http://nces.ed.gov/collegenavigator/)
Davidson	Common Data Set available at www.davidson.edu; U.S. Dept of Education, Institute of Educational Sciences, Nat'l Center for Education Statistics (http://nces.ed.gov/collegenavigator/)
Univ. of Richmond	Common Data Set available at www.richmond.edu; U.S. Dept of Education, Institute of Educational Sciences, Nat'l Center for Education Statistics (http://nces.ed.gov/collegenavigator/)

Index

C

D

E

F

G

H

I

J

L

M

N

O

P

T

U

V

W

Y

Printed in Dunstable, United Kingdom

91220744R00138